RENEWING WORSHIP

D1066730

Life Passages

Marriage, Healing, Funeral

Evangelical Lutheran Church in America
Published by Augsburg Fortress

RENEWING WORSHIP 4
Life Passages: Marriage, Healing, Funeral

This resource has been prepared by the Evangelical Lutheran Church in America for provisional use.

The paper used in this publication meets the minimum requirements of American National Standard for Information Sciences—Permanence of Paper for Printed Library Materials, ANSI Z329.48-1984.

Manufactured in the U.S.A. ISBN 0-8066-7004-5

06 05 04 03 02   1   2   3   4   5

Contents

iv   Preface

vi   Introduction

1   Marriage

23   Healing
Liturgy of Healing   27
Commendation of the Dying   40
Prayer When Life-sustaining Care Ends   45
Confession and Forgiveness: Individual Order   50

57   Funeral
Comforting the Bereaved   63
Funeral Liturgy   66
Committal   72

94   Acknowledgments

97   For Further Reading

100   Evaluation

Preface

In the years since the publication of *Lutheran Book of Worship* in 1978, the pace of change both within the church and beyond has quickened. The past three decades have seen not only a growing ecumenical consensus but also a deepened focus on the church's mission to the world. The church has embraced broadened understandings of culture, increasing musical diversity, changes in the usage of language, a renewed understanding of the central pattern of Christian worship, and an explosion of electronic media and technologies. These shifts have had a profound effect on the weekly assembly gathered around word and sacrament. The present situation calls for a renewal of worship and of common resources for worship, a renewal grounded in the treasures of the church's history while open to the possibilities of the future.

Renewing Worship is a response to these emerging changes in the life of the church and the world. Renewing Worship includes a series of provisional resources intended to provide worship leaders with a range of proposed strategies and materials that address the various liturgical and musical needs of the church. These resources are offered to assist the renewal of corporate worship in a variety of settings, especially among Lutheran churches, in anticipation of the next generation of primary worship resources.

Published beginning in 2001, this series includes hymns and songs (newly written or discovered as well as new approaches to common texts and tunes), liturgical texts and music for weekly and seasonal use, occasional rites (such as marriage, healing, and funeral), resources for daily prayer (morning prayer, evening prayer, and prayer at the close of the day), psalms and canticles, prayers and lectionary texts, and other supporting materials. Over the course of several years, worship leaders will have the opportunity to obtain and evaluate a wide range of Renewing Worship resources both in traditional print format and in electronic form delivered via the Internet at www.renewingworship.org.

These published resources, however, are only one component of the Renewing Worship multiyear plan led by the Evangelical Lutheran Church in America (ELCA) as it enters the next generation of its worship life. Endorsed by the ELCA Church Council and carried out in partnership by the ELCA Division for Congregational Ministries and the Publishing House of the ELCA (Augsburg Fortress), this plan for worship renewal includes five components. The first phase (2001-2002) is a consultative process intended to develop principles for language, music, preaching, and worship space. Related to the ELCA's statement on sacramental practices, *The Use of the Means of Grace*, the outcome of the 2001-2002 consultative process has been published as *Principles for Worship*. These principles are intended to undergird future worship resource development and encourage congregational study, response, and practice.

The second phase (2001-2005) includes a series of editorial teams that collect, develop, and revise worship materials for provisional use. The liturgical and musical resource proposals that emerge from the editorial teams are being published during the third phase of this plan (also in 2001-2005) as trial-use resources in the Renewing Worship series, including the present volume, *Life Passages: Marriage, Healing, Funeral.* These materials include proposals for newly developed, ecumenically shared, or recently revised texts, rites, and music. Crucial to this phase will be careful evaluation and response by congregations and worship leaders based on these proposed strategies and provisional materials.

The fourth phase of the plan includes regional conferences for conversation, resource introduction and evaluation, and congregational feedback. The final phase of the process (2005 and beyond) envisions the drafting of a comprehensive proposal for new primary worship resources designed to succeed *Lutheran Book of Worship.*

As the plan progresses, the shape and parameters of that proposal will continue to unfold. The goal, however, will remain constant: renewing the worship of God in the church as it carries out Christ's mission in a new day.

Introduction

Life Passages: Marriage, Healing, Funeral, the fourth resource in the Renewing Worship series, focuses on the patterns of the people of God as they gather for worship to mark these significant occasions. Each of the three major sections includes core materials that can be used within a eucharistic liturgy or as an independent rite. In addition to the central set of prayers and texts within each rite, supplemental materials provide options that enable these services to be shaped to meet particular pastoral needs and circumstances.

Renewing Worship resources have as one of their foundations *The Use of the Means of Grace,* the statement on the practice of word and sacrament adopted for guidance and practice by the Evangelical Lutheran Church in America in 1997.[1] This introduction includes a summary of that statement's guidance as it relates to the celebration of these occasional services. In this volume, additional support is provided by *Principles for Worship,* which was released in spring 2002 for study and response by the church.[2]

A PASSAGE INITIATED

The course of the Christian life is marked by a variety of passages, although the primary passage is made in the waters of baptism. "In Holy Baptism the Triune God delivers us from the forces of evil, puts our sinful self to death, gives us new birth, adopts us as children, and makes us members of the body of Christ, the Church."[3] Here is the beginning of the passage into life with God in Christ Jesus. Here is the sacrament of our identity as children of God. Although the baptismal bath is a once-in-a-lifetime passage, the sacrament of baptism gives shape to each day of the Christian's life. "By God's gift and call, all of us who have been baptized into Christ Jesus are daily put to death so that we might be raised daily to newness of life."[4]

A PASSAGE SUSTAINED

Once the life of faith is begun through the waters of baptism, no subsequent passage is made alone. All the times and occasions of life are accompanied by the presence of the God made known in Jesus Christ. When Christ commissioned the church to baptize in the triune name, he also promised his continual presence until the end of the age.[5] The presence of Christ through all times and stages of life is revealed in the sacrament of holy communion. "In this sacrament the crucified and risen Christ is present, giving his true body and blood as food and drink."[6] "If baptism is the core of Christian identity, the eucharist is

---

[1] *The Use of the Means of Grace: A Statement on the Practice of Word and Sacrament* (Chicago: Evangelical Lutheran Church in America, 1997).
[2] *Principles for Worship,* Renewing Worship, vol. 2 (Minneapolis: Augsburg Fortress, 2002).
[3] *The Use of the Means of Grace,* principle 14.
[4] *The Use of the Means of Grace,* principle 17.
[5] Matthew 28:20.
[6] *The Use of the Means of Grace,* principle 33.

the continuing enactment of that identity."[7] The gift of this meal strengthens us in faith toward God and in love to one another.[8]

A LIFETIME OF PASSAGES

In the incarnation of Jesus Christ, God embraced human existence and came to know human experience. The incarnate God is the one in whom "we live and move and have our being"[9] and in whom all our passages are made. The church's ministry at marriages, through prayers for healing, and at the time of death grows from the New Testament witness of Christ's own presence at these events. Jesus brought joy to the wedding at Cana, healed the sick as a sign of God's present reign, and proclaimed himself the resurrection and the life at the tomb of Lazarus.

In recent years, some of the church's occasional services have been studied in the larger context of the way humans celebrate life passages by anthropologists such as Arnold van Gennep. He observed events that mark human passages from birth into life, through youth and adolescence, from early adulthood toward maturity, and on to the end of our lives. In his work van Gennep noted three phases that mark these rites of passage: a separation from the old status; liminality—an "in-between" time, and incorporation into a new status.[10] Although such rites of passage may be common to much of human experience, the church marks these times as occasions for grace, and grounds them in the life God gives in baptism. "To accompany people in many of these moments of transition, the Christian community celebrates rites of passage. These rites whereby the Church invokes God's care and providence for people in transition find their efficacy in the power of the Word. . . . It is good that baptism should be often remembered and affirmed in these life-cycle rites."[11]

The joining of two people as one through the exchange of vows and the prayer of blessing, the desire for healing that reaches deeper than medical and technological cure, and the commendation of a loved one from death into eternal life with God are the significant life passages included in this volume. Resources yet to be developed will expand upon the life cycle rites included here. These three central constellations of rites, however, stand as a reminder that all of our passages are made in God. "Where can I go then from your Spirit? Where can I flee from your presence? If I climb up to heaven, you are there; if I make the grave my bed, you are there also."[12]

---

[7] Elaine Ramshaw, *Ritual and Pastoral Care* (Philadelphia: Fortress Press, 1987), 38.

[8] Post-communion prayer, *Lutheran Book of Worship* (Minneapolis: Augsburg Publishing House and Philadelphia: Board of Publication, Lutheran Church in America, 1978), 74.

[9] Acts 17:28.

[10] Arnold van Gennep, *The Rites of Passage*, trans. Monika Vizedom and Gabrielle Caffee (Chicago: University of Chicago Press, 1960).

[11] Chicago Statement on Worship and Culture in *Baptism, Rites of Passage, and Culture*, ed. S. Anita Stauffer (Geneva: Lutheran World Federation, 1999) 1.2.

[12] Psalm 139:6-7 in *Lutheran Book of Worship*, 284.

OCCASIONAL SERVICES AND THE OCCASIONAL CHURCH

When the church names certain rites and liturgies *occasional services* we reveal two things about the nature of such services. They are called occasional because they are celebrated intermittently and not regularly in the same way as the primary Sunday gathering around word and sacrament or scheduled services of daily prayer. They are also called occasional because the rites surrounding marriage, healing, and funerals are prompted by specific occasions. It is the occasion of exchanging vows, of confronting the reality of illness and pain in the name of Christ, or of commending a baptized person to eternal life with God, that prompts the church to gather for these rites.

The assembly that gathers to observe these passages might also be called occasional. Occasional services call together an occasional church. The people who form the assembly bring with them a variety of religious beliefs and spiritual practices; some may be active members of a congregation, others are not. "Whether or not they are members of a faith community, consider themselves freelance Christians, or believe themselves to be spiritual in some fashion, they are nevertheless in relationship with the faithful and will likely be included in family or church functions."[13] In this volume each of the rites includes the possibility of a pastoral introduction. This introduction serves as a type of catechesis and provides a setting for the church's understanding of marriage, healing, or death. The introduction serves to gather a diverse assembly in heart and mind for the occasion.

THE GATHERED AND ACTIVE ASSEMBLY

These rites envision an assembly that is active and participatory rather than merely a gathering of observers at a private event. It is the assembly in its ministry as an assembly that blesses and prays for the couple to be married, that joins the sick in cries of lament and prayers for healing, and that recalls its corporate identity as a people who have already passed from death to life in the waters of baptism as they commend a loved one to God.

"Hymns, liturgy, and creeds are means for the community itself to respond to the Word of God."[14] The assembly's song may need to be more strongly encouraged in settings where occasional services have often relied on music performed only by soloists. Corporate song is one means of unifying the occasional church. "Singing in worship contributes to the formation of the people gathered. Music reflects and shapes the community in its relationship to God."[15]

---

[13] Robert D. Hawkins, "Occasional Services: Border Crossings" in *Inside Out: Worship in an Age of Mission* (Minneapolis: Fortress Press, 1999), 187.
[14] *The Use of the Means of Grace,* application 10A.
[15] "Music and the Christian Assembly" in *Principles for Worship,* principle 11.

Those who preach need to consider the pastoral needs of the whole assembly and not only the needs of the individuals whose specific situation has occasioned the rite. Preaching must take into account the diversity of the assembly gathered as an occasional church and the "myriad of images and stories from popular culture, current affairs, and other religious traditions. These images powerfully shape the minds and spirits of contemporary people."[16] Those who preach to the assembly gathered for a specific occasion "are challenged to find the connections and define the differences between God's story and other stories alive in the culture . . . without altering the essential life-giving message of Jesus Christ."[17]

"The celebration of weddings and funerals within services of Word and Sacrament in the congregation are appropriate traditions."[18] The rites for healing in this volume also include the celebration of holy communion as the context for the ministry of healing, whether in a large assembly or a gathering of two or three. Because of the diversity of the assembly gathered for occasional services, it is important to articulate the practice of eucharistic hospitality:

> Invitation to the sacrament is by invitation of the Lord, presented through the church to those who are baptized. It is a sign of hospitality to provide a brief written or oral statement in worship that teaches Christ's presence in the sacrament. This assists guests to decide whether they wish to accept the Lord's invitation. In the exercise of this hospitality, it is wise for our congregations to be sensitive to the eucharistic practices of the churches from which visitors may come. When a wedding or funeral occurs during a celebration of Holy Communion, communion is offered to all baptized persons.[19]

LIFE PASSAGES AND THE MISSION OF THE CHURCH

"In every celebration of the means of grace, God acts to show forth both the need of the world and the truth of the Gospel. In every gathering of Christians around the proclaimed Word and the holy sacraments, God acts to empower the Church for mission."[20] The rites for life passages are also a part of the mission of the church. Through its worship at times of marriage, healing, and death the church articulates its beliefs about the nature of relationships bound by promise, about healing and wholeness in Jesus Christ, and about death and life. At transitional life events "questions about ultimate meaning and purposefulness arise. At such critical moments, the stranger and Christian alike, out of fear, anger, despair, or hope, ask where God is in the midst of the turmoil."[21] These rites are one way for the church to declare the hope that is within us.[22]

---

[16] "Preaching and the Christian Assembly" in *Principles for Worship,* application 14F.
[17] "Preaching and the Christian Assembly" in *Principles for Worship,* applications 14G and 14H.
[18] *The Use of the Means of Grace,* application 13A.
[19] *The Use of the Means of Grace,* principle 49, applications 49A and 49B.
[20] *The Use of the Means of Grace,* 51.
[21] Hawkins, 191.
[22] 1 Peter 3:15.

CONTINUING PASSAGES

Although this volume of rites includes selected materials related to three major times of life passage, the limited scope of this collection is a reminder that no resource can take into consideration all the stages that mark human life. "All aspects of life, home and school, community and nation, daily work and leisure, citizenship and friendship, belong to God."[23]

The passages that individuals, families, and congregations might want to mark are many and will change with time and circumstance. Those who are responsible for the ministry of word and sacrament use and build upon the church's occasional rites to meet the needs of various circumstances. For example, the rite for affirmation of baptism is a valuable and powerful guide in many pastoral situations. Any rite of passage, any change of the direction of one's life, is marked by a return to the passage with Christ through the waters of baptism.

When there are changes in a Christian's life, rites of affirmation of baptism and intercessory prayer could mark the passage. Moving into a nursing home, beginning parenthood or grandparenthood, choosing or changing an occupation, moving out of the parental home, the diagnosis of a chronic illness, the end of one's first year of mourning, the ending of a relationship, and retirement are all examples of life's transitions that could be acknowledged by these rites. Other examples include adoption and the naming of an already baptized child, release from prison, reunion of an immigrant family, and new life after abuse or addiction.[24]

RENEWING WORSHIP: FOUNDATIONAL PATTERNS, FLEXIBLE RITES

Each of the provisional rites in this volume offers both a foundational pattern for the rite and a number of resources that can be used in flexible ways to fill out the rite within particular seasons and contexts. Each rite is accompanied by an outline of the elements of the rite and a narrative description of its major movements ("Shape of the Rite"). Primary or core elements of the rite are designated by letters in bold, together with supportive elements of the rite in regular type.

Most of the rites include a few alternatives within the body of the rites, which are further supplemented by a section of additional and seasonal texts. This presentation—the essential shape of the rite, the core liturgy with texts and instructions, and a collection of supplemental texts—is intended to enrich and expand the celebration of these rites without obscuring what is central. Rites can be simple, transparent, accessible, and at the same time offer great variety and flexibility.

---

[23] *The Use of the Means of Grace,* background 52A.
[24] *The Use of the Means of Grace,* application 30A.

RENEWING WORSHIP: MARRIAGE

The marriage service, unlike prayers for healing and wholeness or the rite for funerals, is not a passage that will be undertaken by everyone. For those who choose this passage, the church is present to proclaim God's saving and redeeming word and pray for God's blessing on two people now made one.

Classic Lutheran theology has long understood the union of a man and a woman in marriage as an order of creation and a gift from God. In such a view, one does not speak of a Christian marriage. Rather, one speaks of marriage between Christians.[25] At the same time however, Lutheran marriage rites have invoked the presence of Christ our redeemer, spoken of marriage together with eschatological joy, and looked to the couple as a sign of God's faithful covenant with the people.

The marriage liturgy presented here takes its shape primarily from an ecumenical rite produced by the Consultation on Common Texts.[26] The shape of this rite not only reflects the broad ecumenical consensus of our day; it is also present in earlier generations of Lutheran rites. In addition, the shape of this rite is a centuries-old pattern among English-speaking Christians, and so it resonates with many cultural expectations of marriage services. Several aspects of this rite stand in contrast to the rite in *Lutheran Book of Worship*:

- ▶ A pastoral *introduction* at the beginning of the service provides a setting for the church's understanding of marriage and gathers the assembly in heart and mind for the occasion. It recounts God's gift of marriage in creation, the union of a couple as an image of Christ's union with the church, and the continued presence of Christ through the Holy Spirit.

- ▶ The *declaration of intention* stands on its own, whereas in *Lutheran Book of Worship* it was collapsed into one act with the exchange of vows. The giving of consent at the beginning of the service and at the door of the church is as old as Luther's marriage order of 1529.[27] Here the couple's declaration is placed at the beginning of the service and is separated from the vows in order to distinguish what is preliminary from what is central.

---

[25] See Philip Pfatteicher, *Commentary on the Lutheran Book of Worship* (Minneapolis: Augsburg Fortress, 1990), 455-473.
[26] Consultation on Common Texts, *A Christian Celebration of Marriage* (Minneapolis: Augsburg Fortress, 1995).
[27] Martin Luther, "The Order of Marriage for Common Pastors" in *Luther's Works,* Volume 53 (Philadelphia: Fortress Press, 1965), 111.

▶ Both the *family and the gathered assembly* declare their support and blessing. While the practice of "giving away the bride" at the beginning of the service has appropriately faded from use, the ritual need for families to offer their support as the rite begins has not. Unlike *Lutheran Book of Worship,* which offered the possibility of a blessing from family and wedding party following the exchange of vows and rings, this declaration is located at the beginning of the rite immediately following the couple's declaration and prior to the prayer of the day.

▶ A *nuptial blessing* follows the vows, exchange of rings, and acclamation of the marriage. This blessing is shaped after other great prayers of blessing used in the life of the church. It praises God for creation and for the love made visible in Jesus Christ. It invokes the Holy Spirit to make that same love known in the life of the couple now joined as one. Using strong and vivid images, it prays for God's blessing in all aspects of the life of the couple.

▶ The *intercessions* that follow the blessing are structured in the same familiar way as intercessory prayers of a Sunday assembly rather than the solemn collects included in *Lutheran Book of Worship.* It is best if they are crafted for the specific needs of the occasion; however, several sets of prayers are included here as examples. Just as the nuptial blessing prayed for the couple to be a sign of God's love in the world, these intercessions move the rite from exclusive focus on the couple to the various needs of the assembly and the world.

▶ Several texts are included here for use when a celebration of *holy communion* is the context for the rite for marriage.

RENEWING WORSHIP: HEALING

Illness of body or spirit is an unavoidable passage for human beings. Illness disrupts the regular patterns of life and, when it is serious, threatens our future and our hope. Because illness often alters the relationship of a person with other people, it has social as well as physical consequences.[28] "When we call on Jesus as the Christ for healing, we appeal to what is close to his heart: concern for those who suffer because of physical illness and other afflictions of the human spirit."[29] When the church prays for healing, it embraces God's gift offered in and through the medical community. At the same time, the church's ministry of healing moves deeper than the hope for a medical or technological cure. The biblical word for healing carries with it additional meanings of salvation, wholeness, and peace with God.

---

[28] Jennifer Glen c.c.v.i., "Rites of Healing: A Reflection in Pastoral Theology" in *Alternative Futures for Worship, Volume 7, Anointing of the Sick,* (Collegeville: The Liturgical Press, 1987).
[29] Chicago Statement on Worship and Culture, 3.1.

The provisional service proposed here is easily adaptable to a wide range of congregational and personal circumstances. It may be used in the context of a celebration of holy communion within a large assembly or it may be used as a service of word and prayer in a small gathering of two or three. It may be used in the building in which a congregation regularly meets or it may be used at the bedside of a critically ill person. In any circumstance, this rite offers anointing, laying on of hands, and prayer as the central actions in the church's ministry of healing.

▶ The *introduction* entrusts to God's care all who are in need of healing and hope. In a large assembly this introduction may be used during the gathering to underscore the church's practice of healing as people prepare for worship. In a small gathering of family or friends around an individual who is ill, the introduction may serve the mission of the church and proclaim our hope to people who are at the margins of church life. In the presence of two or three others, it may be adapted to speak directly to the pastoral needs of the one who is ill.

▶ The *litany* includes a simple rhythm and a repeated refrain to assist assembly participation without the need for a printed resource.

▶ Although some synods sponsor annual liturgies in which oils are blessed for use by congregations in baptism and anointing of the sick, this rite includes a prayer for the *blessing of oil* for use in other situations. A stock, a small container holding oil, may be convenient in homes or clinical settings. In larger gatherings, especially within churches, a vessel that allows the oil to be seen may be used. This oil could then be poured into a smaller bowl for use during the anointing.[30]

▶ "*Anointing, hand-laying, and the prayer of faith*, whenever possible in the presence of the community, are the core elements of Christian rites of healing. They are handed down to us by apostolic tradition. (Mark 6:13; Mark 16:17-18; James 5:14-15)."[31]

▶ A number of texts are included to assist in the celebration of rites of healing within the context of *holy communion*.

▶ *Commendation of the Dying* is included within the rites for healing as a way to entrust the dying to final peace, wholeness, healing, and salvation in Christ. *Prayer When Life-Sustaining Care Ends* offers resources for circumstances that have become more common as the capacities of medical technology have continued to evolve.

---

[30] Paul R. Nelson, "The Ministry of Healing" in *Sunday and Seasons 2001* (Minneapolis: Augsburg Fortress, 2000).
[31] Chicago Statement on Worship and Culture, 3.2.

▶ *Confession and Forgiveness* for use with an individual penitent is included in this section. Spiritual healing of the brokenness of sin is a gift associated with the church's practice of individual confession and absolution. In particular pastoral circumstances, this rite, or a corporate order of confession and forgiveness,[32] may also be used in conjunction with rites of healing and commendation of the dying.

RENEWING WORSHIP: FUNERAL

Death is the passage that is undertaken by every human being. It is the culmination of all human life passages and the fulfillment of the initiatory passage of baptism. "This significance of baptism—the dying or drowning of sin—is not fulfilled completely in this life. Indeed this does not happen until one passes through bodily death. . . . Only then will that be finished which the lifting up out of baptism signifies. . . . Then shall we be truly lifted up out of baptism and be completely born, and we shall put on the true baptismal garment of immortal life in heaven."[33]

This provisional funeral liturgy carries forward the essential aspects of the rites in *LBW* and *Occasional Services*. Several additional developments may be noted.

▶ The prayers for *Comforting the Bereaved* are the beginning of the series of funeral rites. This rite is an important aspect of the church's ministry at the time of death and deserves greater accessibility.

▶ This service takes note of the growing cultural acceptance and practice of *cremation*. The term coffin is defined here to include also an urn or ossuary, and several of the prayers offer particular options for the situation of cremation.

▶ The oldest memory in the church's care for the dead includes the celebration of the *Lord's Supper,* and so eucharistic propers are provided with this rite. "As a means of grace Holy Communion is that messianic banquet at which God bestows mercy and forgiveness, creates and strengthens faith . . . and provides a sure and certain hope for the coming resurrection to eternal life."[34]

▶ The pastoral *introduction* declares God's promise of new life through baptism into Christ while the coffin is being covered with a pall. An option for *sprinkling* the coffin recalls those same baptismal promises for the person who has died.

---

[32] See *Holy Baptism and Related Rites*, Renewing Worship, Volume 3 (Minneapolis: Augsburg Fortress, 2002).
[33] Martin Luther, "The Holy and Blessed Sacrament of Baptism" in *Luther's Works*, Volume 35 (Philadelphia: Fortress Press, 1965), 30-31.
[34] *The Use of the Means of Grace*, principle 54.

▶ The *prayer of the day* includes a number of new collects and provides options for a broad range of pastoral circumstances.

▶ The rite acknowledges the possibility for *remembrances* offered by family or friends after the prayer of the day or before the commendation and farewell.

▶ At the *commendation*, the presiding minister invites the congregation into a period of silence before the prayer. This takes the cultural element of marking a moment of silence for those who have died and gives room to speak the church's faith that in death we are entrusted to the eternal care of God. As with the prayer of the day, a number of options for the commendation speak to a broad range of pastoral needs.

▶ A song of farewell may be sung following the commendation. "Now, Lord, you let your servant go in peace" served as a song of farewell in earlier Lutheran rites and is offered again in this provisional rite. In addition, a song that reflects ecumenical use, "Into paradise," is included here.

▶ The *committal* may be adapted for a wide range of circumstances. In some cases, burial immediately follows the rite in the church. In other cases, both distance and time separate burial from the celebration of word and sacrament. When the committal immediately concludes the service, a long pastoral introduction, extended scripture passages, and the Lord's Prayer may be redundant. When the committal happens at a later time or distant location, a fuller rite of committal may be desired.

▶ The *sending* is a responsive litany and is easily remembered and prayed without the need of a printed resource for those who have gathered at the burial site.

Supplemental resources include alternative prayers for a wide range of circumstances, including the death of a child (with special attention to the stillborn child), a death by violence, and a death by suicide.

FUTURE DEVELOPMENT OF LIFE PASSAGE RESOURCES

At several places in the provisional resources of this volume, reference is made to additional prayers and other materials that are proposed for further development. For example, the preparation of a comprehensive set of scripture readings, psalms, prayers, and blessings for use in the church's ministry of healing is a continuing area of development. Rites such as the blessing of a civil marriage or the observance of a marriage anniversary will also be prepared. An important aspect of the feedback needed from those who make provisional use of this resource is the identification of such future areas of development.

USING THIS RESOURCE

This collection is intended for provisional use among congregations of the Evangelical Lutheran Church in America and beyond. Worship leaders are encouraged to consider a congregation's history and worship practices before introducing new materials.

Materials in this collection are designed for provisional use in worship. Electronic files of selected materials are also available for download (www.renewingworship.org) and placement in congregational worship folders.

QUESTIONS OF COPYRIGHT

As a whole, the texts and arrangement of materials in *Life Passages: Marriage, Healing, and Funeral* are covered under copyright (although individual items may be in the public domain or used here by arrangement with other publishers).

Permission is granted to reproduce copies for local one-time, congregational use until December 31, 2005. Information regarding this provision and the required copyright notice is included on page ii of this resource.

EVALUATION

An essential goal of Renewing Worship is the evaluation of strategies and content proposals by worshiping congregations and their leaders. Included in each printed volume as well as on the website (www.renewingworship.org) is an evaluation form that addresses the strategies employed in each volume of the series. Feedback received will help to shape the subsequent stages of the process toward new worship materials.

Marriage

Shape of the Rite

Marriage is a gift of God, intended for the joy and strength of those who enter it and for the well-being of the whole human family. In creation God blessed humankind with mutual companionship, the capacity to love, and the care and nurture of children. God's faithfulness, enacted in the covenant with the people Israel, is the promise in which marriage, too, is grounded. Jesus affirmed the covenant of marriage and, by the mystery of his self-giving, revealed the height and depth of love. Even as the one Spirit holds the church of God in the bond of peace, so the Holy Spirit sustains those who are united in marriage, that as one they may be a living sign of God's grace, love, and fidelity.

GATHERING
Entrance
Greeting
Introduction
Declaration of Intention
Prayer of the Day

The marriage liturgy is a service of worship in which the promises of marriage are made before God and the Christian assembly. Those gathered represent the whole people of God and at the same time include people who bring a variety of religious beliefs and spiritual practices. Music and an entrance procession often begin this liturgy, as those who enter symbolize the gathering of all present into worship. After the greeting, a pastoral introduction is an occasion to highlight the church's understanding of marriage and draw the people together in heart and mind. Those to be married are the primary ministers of the wedding; ordained clergy serve as official witnesses and preside during the liturgical celebration. As the assembly gathers, the couple declares their intention to marry. As active participants in the liturgy, the family and the gathered assembly may be asked to offer their support and blessing. The gathering rite ends with the prayer of the day, as the assembly prepares to hear the word of God.

WORD
Readings
Responses
Sermon
Hymn of the Day

Scripture readings declare the steadfast love of God, proclaim the blessings of God, and call the couple to live out God's love within the covenant of their life together. Additional readings from the lectionary may also be considered to reflect themes of covenant and love associated with particular times of the church's year. Members of the family, the wedding party, or the assembly may be invited to proclaim the readings in order to express the corporate nature of this liturgy. Psalms, hymns, and songs provide additional ways to proclaim and respond to the word of God.

MARRIAGE
Vows
Giving of Rings
Acclamation
Nuptial Blessing
Intercessions

At the center of the marriage liturgy stand the exchange of vows by the couple and the gift of God's blessing. The faithfulness promised in the vows is grounded in God's unfailing faithfulness as expressed in the promise of baptism. The exchange of rings is a visual and tangible symbol reinforcing the words of promise. Any additional symbolic acts should support rather than overshadow the vows and the primary symbol of the giving of rings. The marriage, enacted through word and symbol, is announced and acclaimed by the presiding minister and the whole assembly. In the nuptial blessing the presiding minister blesses God for the gifts of creation and covenant, gives thanks for salvation in Christ, and invokes the Holy Spirit that these same blessings may be made known in and through the newly married couple. Prayers of intercession follow the blessing: as God's mercy is invoked for the whole world, the focus of the rite shifts from the couple to the ministry that all share with one another in the world. When the sacrament of holy communion is not celebrated, the service continues with the Lord's Prayer, blessing, dismissal, and departure.

[MEAL]

Marriage and the eucharist are both covenants, characterized by self-giving love. Marriage reveals self-giving love at the heart of a relationship between two people joined as one. Holy communion makes present the self-giving love of Jesus Christ in his body and blood through the sacrament. The assembly, gathered around two people and their union as one flesh, now gathers around the love of God and the union of human and divine in Jesus Christ. When marriage is celebrated within the liturgy of word and meal, communion is offered to all baptized persons.

SENDING
Blessing
Dismissal
Departure

As in other services of worship, this service ends simply. Together with the newly married couple, all receive the blessing of God, are invited to leave in peace, and are sent out to serve in word and deed bearing the good news of the love of God made known in Jesus Christ.

MARRIAGE

Outline

GATHERING
Entrance
Greeting
Introduction
Declaration of Intention
Prayer of the Day

WORD
Readings
Responses
Sermon
Hymn of the Day

MARRIAGE
Vows
Giving of Rings
Acclamation
Nuptial Blessing
Intercessions

[MEAL]

SENDING
Blessing
Dismissal
Departure

MARRIAGE

GATHERING

ENTRANCE

A hymn may be sung during the entrance, or other music may be played.

GREETING

The presiding minister greets the assembly:
The grace of our Lord Jesus Christ, the love of God,
and the communion of the Holy Spirit be with you all.
And also with you.

INTRODUCTION

The minister may introduce the rite with these or similar words:
A p. 12 ►
Dear friends: We have come together in the presence of God to witness the marriage of
name and *name*, to surround them with our prayers, and to share in their joy.

The scriptures teach us that the bond and covenant of marriage is a gift of God, a holy
mystery in which two become one flesh, an image of the union of Christ and the church.
As *name* and *name* give themselves to each other today, we remember that at Cana in
Galilee our Lord Jesus Christ made the wedding feast a sign of God's reign of love.

Let us enter into this celebration confident that, through the Holy Spirit, Christ is present
with us now also; we pray that this couple may fulfill God's purpose for the whole of
their lives.

DECLARATION OF INTENTION

The minister addresses the couple, asking each person in turn:
A p. 13 ►
Name, will you have *name* to be your *wife/husband*,
to live together in a holy marriage?
Will you love *her/him*, comfort *her/him*, honor and keep *her/him*,
in sickness and in health,
and, forsaking all others, be faithful to *her/him*
as long as you both shall live?
Response: I will.

The minister says to the families:

A p. 13 ▸

Will you, the families of *name* and *name*, give your love and blessing to this new family?
The families respond: We will.

The minister says to the assembly:
Will all of you, by God's grace, do everything in your power
to uphold and care for these two persons in their life together?
We will.

PRAYER OF THE DAY

The presiding minister leads the prayer of the day:

A p. 14 ▸

Let us pray.
Eternal God, our creator and redeemer,
as you gladdened the wedding at Cana in Galilee
by the presence of your Son,
so bring your joy to this wedding by his presence now.
Look in favor upon *name* and *name*
and grant that they, rejoicing in all your gifts,
may at length celebrate the unending marriage feast with Christ our Lord,
who lives and reigns with you and the Holy Spirit,
one God, now and forever.
Amen.

WORD

READINGS and RESPONSES

*Two or three readings are proclaimed. When communion is celebrated, the last is a reading from
the gospels. A psalm may be sung or said in response to a reading from the Old Testament. A sung
acclamation may precede the reading of the gospel.*

SERMON

Silence for reflection follows.

HYMN OF THE DAY

A hymn of the day may be sung.

MARRIAGE

VOWS

The presiding minister addresses the couple in these or similar words:
Name and *name*,
I invite you to join your hands and declare your vows.

The couple join hands. Speaking so that all can hear, each says to the other the following or similar
words; the minister may help them proclaim their vows:
A   *pp. 14–15* ▶
In the presence of God and this community,
I, *name*, take you, *name*, to be my *wife/husband*;
to have and to hold from this day forward,
in joy and in sorrow,
in plenty and in want,
in sickness and in health,
to love and to cherish,
as long as we both shall live.
This is my solemn vow.

GIVING OF RINGS

When rings are to be exchanged, they may be placed on the service book of the minister or held by
an assisting minister. The presiding minister may say:
A   *p. 15* ▶
Bless these rings, O God;
may they who wear them live in love and fidelity,
and continue in your service all the days of their lives,
through Jesus Christ our Lord.
Amen.

The couple exchange rings with these or similar words:
A   *p. 15* ▶
Name, I give you this ring as a sign of my love and faithfulness.

ACCLAMATION

The presiding minister addresses the assembly:
Name and *name*,
by their promises before God and in the presence of this assembly,
have bound themselves to one another as husband and wife.
Those whom God has joined together let no one put asunder.
Amen. Thanks be to God.

A sung acclamation, hymn, or other music may follow in response to the announcement of marriage.
Other symbols of marriage may be given or used at this time.

NUPTIAL BLESSING

The couple may kneel as the presiding minister prays for God's blessing:

A   pp. 16–17 ▶

We give you thanks, most gracious God,
for in your great love you created us male and female
and made the union of husband and wife
an image of the covenant between you and your people.
You sent Jesus Christ to come among us,
making your love visible in him, to bring new life to the world.

Send your Holy Spirit to pour out the abundance of your blessing on *name* and *name*,
who have this day given themselves to each other in marriage.

Bless them in their work and in their companionship;
in their sleeping and in their waking;
in their joys and in their sorrows;
in their life and in their death.
Let their love for each other be a seal upon their hearts,
a mantle about their shoulders, and a crown upon their foreheads.

Bless them so that all may see in their lives together
within the community of your people
a vision of your kingdom on earth.
And finally, in the fullness of time,
welcome them into the glory of your presence.

Through your Son Jesus Christ
with the Holy Spirit in your holy church
all honor and glory is yours, almighty Father, now and forever.
Amen.

INTERCESSIONS

Prayers of intercession for the world and its needs are prayed. These prayers, prepared or adapted for the particular occasion, may include the following or similar petitions. An assisting minister may lead the prayers:

A   pp. 17–18 ▶

Seeing how greatly God has loved us, let us pray for the whole world.

For the Christian community everywhere;
for the life and ministry of the baptized,
and for pastors, leaders, and servants of the gospel,
that the church may be the risen body of Christ in the world.
O God, source of all life,
hear our prayer.

For all communities everywhere;
for our nation, for all those who govern and for all in authority,
and for justice and peace throughout the world.
O God, source of all life,
hear our prayer.

For those we love easily, and for those with whom we struggle,
for those different from us and for those familiar to us,
that we might be instruments of God's peace.
O God, source of all life,
hear our prayer.

For those who suffer in any way, and those who are lonely,
for the sick, the dying, and those who are bereaved,
for those who are poor, hungry, homeless, or unemployed,
for the victims of violence, hatred, and intolerance.
O God, source of all life,
hear our prayer.

For all those who are bound to us in love;
for our families, friends, and neighbors,
remembering also all who have gone before us (especially *name/s*).
O God, source of all life,
hear our prayer.

Other intercessions may be added. The presiding minister concludes the prayers:
Creator of all,
you make us in your image and likeness
and fill us with everlasting life.
Hear the prayers of your people
and grant to *name* and *name* grace to live in unity and joy
all the days of their lives.
We ask this through Jesus Christ, in the Holy Spirit,
to whom, with you, one God, be praise forever and ever.
Amen.

When holy communion is not celebrated, the Lord's Prayer follows. The liturgy concludes with the sending rite on page 10.

MEAL

When holy communion is celebrated, the liturgy continues with the greeting of peace and the remainder of the liturgy of the meal.

After the communion, an assisting minister may lead the following or a similar prayer:

PRAYER AFTER COMMUNION

Loving God,
we thank you that you have fed us in this holy meal,
united us with Christ,
and given us a foretaste of the marriage feast of the Lamb.
So strengthen us in your service that our daily lives may show our thanks,
through Jesus Christ our Lord.
Amen.

SENDING

GREETING OF PEACE

When it has not been included earlier in the liturgy, the greeting of peace may be shared, beginning with this dialogue between the presiding minister and the assembly:
The peace of the Lord be with you always.
And also with you.
The couple may greet each other with a kiss. All present may greet one another with a gesture of peace, using these or similar words: Peace be with you.

BLESSING

The presiding minister blesses the assembly:
A
p. 19 ►
God Almighty send you light and truth
to keep you all the days of your life.
The hand of God protect you;
the holy angels accompany you;
and the blessing of almighty God,
the Father, the ✛ Son, and the Holy Spirit,
be with you now and forever.
Amen.

DISMISSAL

An assisting minister may send the assembly forth:
Go in peace. Serve the Lord.
Thanks be to God.

DEPARTURE

A hymn may be sung or instrumental music played as the wedding party leaves the church.

Scripture Readings

OLD TESTAMENT

Genesis 1:26-28	*Woman and man created in the image of God*
Genesis 2:18-24	*Companionship rather than loneliness*
Proverbs 3:3-6	*Loyalty and faithfulness written on the heart*
Song of Solomon 2:10-13	*The voice of the beloved*
Song of Solomon 8:6-7	*Many waters cannot quench love*
Isaiah 63:7-9	*God's steadfast love lifts up the people*
Jeremiah 31:31-34	*The new covenant of the people of God*

PSALM

Psalm 67	*May God be merciful to us and bless us*
Psalm 100	*We are God's people and the sheep of God's pasture*
Psalm 117	*The steadfast love of the Lord*
Psalm 121	*The Lord keeps watch over you*
Psalm 127	*Unless the Lord builds the house*
Psalm 128	*Blessed are those who walk in the Lord's ways*
Psalm 150	*Let everything that breathes praise the Lord*

NEW TESTAMENT

Romans 8:31-35, 37-39	*If God is for us, who is against us*
Romans 12:1-2, 9-18	*A living sacrifice and genuine love*
1 Corinthians 12:31—13:13	*The greatest gift is love*
Ephesians 3:14-19	*The breadth, length, height and depth of Christ's love*
Ephesians 5:1-2, 21-33	*Walk in love, as Christ loved us*
Philippians 4:4-9	*Rejoice in the Lord always*
Colossians 3:12-17	*Clothed in compassion, kindness, meekness and patience*
1 John 3:18-24	*Let us love in truth and action*
1 John 4:7-16	*Let us love one another for love is of God*

GOSPEL

Matthew 5:1-10	*The beatitudes*
Matthew 5:14-16	*You are the light, let your light shine*
Matthew 7:21, 24-29	*A wise person builds upon the rock*
Matthew 19:3-6	*What God has united must not be divided*
Matthew 22:35-40	*Love, the greatest commandment*
Mark 10:6-9	*They are no longer two but one*
John 2:1-11	*The wedding at Cana*
John 15:9-17	*Love one another as I have loved you*

Supplemental Materials

The following texts may be used as alternatives or supplements to those included in the rite.

INTRODUCTION

B

<u>Name</u> and <u>name</u> have come to make their marriage vows
in the presence of God and of this congregation.
Let us now witness their promises to each other
and surround them with our prayers,
giving thanks to God for the gift of marriage
and asking God's blessing upon them,
so that they may be strengthened for their life together
and nurtured in their love for God.

We rejoice that marriage is given by God,
blessed by our Lord Jesus Christ,
and sustained by the Holy Spirit.
Therefore, let marriage be held in honor by all.

C

The Lord God in goodness created us male and female,
and by the gift of marriage founded human community
in a joy that begins now and is brought to perfection in the life to come.

Because of sin, our age-old rebellion,
the gladness of marriage can be overcast
and the gift of the family can become a burden.
But because God, who established marriage,
continues still to bless it with abundant and ever-present support,
we can be sustained in our weariness and have our joy restored.

D

Beloved people of God,
we have come together in the presence of God
to witness and bless the covenant of love and fidelity
<u>name</u> and <u>name</u> are to make with each other.

The union of two persons in heart, body, and mind
is intended by God for their mutual joy,
for the help and comfort given one another in prosperity and adversity;
and that their love may be a blessing to all whom they encounter.
This solemn covenant is not to be entered into unadvisedly or lightly,
but reverently, deliberately,
and with the commitment to seek God's will for their lives.

DECLARATION OF INTENTION

Couple

B

Name, will you receive *name* as your *wife/husband*
and bind yourself to *her/him* in the covenant of marriage?
Will you promise to love and honor *her/him* in true devotion,
to rejoice with *her/him* in times of gladness,
to grieve with *her/him* in times of sorrow,
and to be faithful to *her/him* as long as you both shall live?
Response: I will, with the help of God.

C

Name, living in the promise of God,
joined to Christ in your baptism,
will you give yourself to *name* in love and faithfulness?
Will you share your life with *her/him*,
in joy and in sorrow, in health and in sickness,
for richer, for poorer, for better, for worse,
and will you be faithful to *her/him* as long as you both shall live?
Response: I will, with the help of God.

DECLARATION OF INTENTION

Assembly

B

The minister says to the assembly:
Families, friends, and all those gathered here with *name* and *name*,
will you promise to support and care for them in their life together,
to sustain and pray for them in times of trouble,
to give thanks with them in times of joy,
to honor the bonds of their covenant,
and to affirm the love of God reflected in their lives?
We will, with the help of God.

C

*When pastorally appropriate, one or both of these questions may be used when children are
brought into the family of those to be married.*

The minister may ask the couple:
Name and *name*, will you be faithful and loving parents to *name/s*?
Response: We will, with the help of God.

The minister may ask the children:
Name/s, will you help *name* and *name* in their marriage?
Response: We will, with the help of God.

PRAYER OF THE DAY

B

Gracious God,
you sent your Son Jesus Christ into the world
to reveal your love to all people.
Enrich *name* and *name* with every good gift,
that their life together may show forth your love;
and grant that at the last we may all celebrate with Christ
the marriage feast that has no ending;
in the name of Jesus Christ our Lord.
Amen.

C

Eternal God, creator and sustainer of us all,
give your grace to *name* and *name*.
Grant that in the years ahead
they may be faithful to the vows they make this day,
and that in the strength of the Holy Spirit
they may grow together in the love, joy, and peace
of our Savior Jesus Christ.
Amen.

GOSPEL ACCLAMATION

Alleluia. Blessed are they
who walk in the ways of the Lord. Alleluia.

VOWS

B

I take you, *name*, to be my *wife/husband* from this day forward,
to join with you and share all that is to come,
and I promise to be faithful to you
until death parts us.

C

I, *name*, give myself to you, *name*.
By the grace of God,
I promise to support and care for you.
In the love of Christ,
I promise to love and cherish you.
With the Spirit's help,
I promise to be faithful to you,
as long as we both shall live.

D

I take you, _name_, to be my *wife/husband,*
and these things I promise you:
I will be faithful to you and honest with you;
I will respect, trust, help, and care for you;
I will forgive you as we have been forgiven;
and I will share my life with you,
through the best and worst of all that is to come,
until death parts us.

GIVING OF RINGS

Prayer

B

Gracious God, by your blessing
let these rings be to _name_ and _name_
a symbol of their unending love and faithfulness,
to remind them of the vow and covenant they have made this day,
through Jesus Christ our Lord.
Amen.

C

We give you thanks, O God of grace,
for your love and faithfulness to your people.
Bless these rings,
that they may be symbols of the enduring commitment
name and _name_ have made to each other;
through Jesus Christ our Savior.
Amen.

GIVING OF RINGS

Exchange of Rings

B

Name, I give you this ring as a symbol of my vow.
With all that I am, and all that I have, I honor you,
in the name of the Father, and of the Son, and of the Holy Spirit.

ACCLAMATION

A

Your love, O Lord, forever will we sing,
for your faithfulness endures from age to age.

B

God is love;
let us love one another as God first loved us.

C

May you dwell in God's presence forever;
may true and constant love preserve you.

D

May the blessing of God
set a seal on your hearts
to strengthen you in faithfulness and love.

NUPTIAL BLESSING

B

When a prayer for children is desired, the following words may be included in the blessing immediately before "Let their love for each other be a seal upon their hearts":
Give them the gift and heritage of children in accordance with your will,
and make their home a haven of peace.

C

When children are brought into the family of the newly married couple, the following words may be included in the blessing immediately before "Let their love for each other be a seal upon their hearts":
You have given them the gift and heritage of children;
make their home a haven of peace.

D

Most gracious God, we give you thanks
for your tender love in sending Jesus Christ
to come among us, to be born of a human mother,
and to make the way of the cross to be the way of life.

By the power of your Holy Spirit,
pour out your abundant blessing upon *name* and *name*.
Defend them from every enemy.
Lead them into all peace.
Let their love for each other be a seal upon their hearts,
a mantle about their shoulders, and a crown upon their foreheads.

Bless them in their work and in their companionship;
in their sleeping and in their waking;
in their joys and in their sorrows;
in their life and in their death.

Finally in your mercy, bring them to that table
where your saints feast forever in your banquet;
through Jesus Christ our Lord,
who with you and the Holy Spirit lives and reigns,
one God, now and forever.
Amen.

E
The Lord God, who created our first parents
and established them in marriage,
establish and sustain you, that you may find delight in each other
and grow in holy love until your life's end.
Amen.

INTERCESSIONS

B
On this day of rejoicing,
let us bless God for divine love made flesh in Jesus Christ.

We praise you, O God,
for the joy that *name* and *name* have found in each other
and pray that the strength of their love
may reflect your gracious love and enrich our common life.
Gracious and tender God,
hear our prayer.

From your great store of strength give them power and patience,
affection and understanding, courage,
and love toward you, toward each other, and toward the world.
Gracious and tender God,
hear our prayer.

Make them gentle and patient, ready to trust each other,
and, when they fail, willing to acknowledge their fault
and to give and receive forgiveness.
Gracious and tender God,
hear our prayer.

Use us to support *name* and *name* in their lives together.
Give us such a sense of your constant love
that we may employ all our strength in a life of praise of you.
Gracious and tender God,
hear our prayer.

Strengthen and bless friends and family gathered here,
call to mind those separated by distance,
console those who mourn the loss of loved ones,
and be present with those for whom love is a stranger.
Gracious and tender God,
hear our prayer.

Look graciously on the world you have made
and for which your Son gave his life.
Defend and guide all who suffer want or anxiety.
Gracious and tender God,
hear our prayer.

We praise you, merciful God, for the saints,
those who have died in Christ (especially *name/s*).
Strengthen us by their example
and bring us all to the marriage feast of the Lamb.
Gracious and tender God,
hear our prayer.

The presiding minister concludes the prayers:
Most gracious God, you have made us in your image
and given us over to one another's care.
Hear the prayers of your people,
that unity may overcome division,
hope vanquish despair,
and joy conquer sorrow;
through our Lord Jesus Christ.
Amen.

PROPER PREFACE

It is indeed right and salutary
that we should at all times and in all places offer thanks and praise,
O Lord, almighty and ever-living God.
You made us in your image;
male and female you created us.
You give us the gift of marriage
and call us to reflect your faithfulness
as we serve one another in the bond of covenant love.
And so, with the church on earth and the hosts of heaven,
we praise your name and join their unending hymn:
The Sanctus follows.

BLESSING

B
The blessed and holy Trinity
make you strong in faith and love,
defend you on every side,
and guide you in truth and peace,
now and forever.
Amen.

Notes on the Rite

GENERAL

The marriage liturgy is normally preceded by a period of preparation. Preferably beginning at least six months before the marriage, this time of preparation may involve those to be married in conversation and counsel with the pastor and with other couples regarding the liturgy of marriage and the gifts and responsibilities of marriage. During this time of preparation, an announcement of an upcoming wedding may be communicated within a congregation, using a form such as this: "_Name_ and _name_ have announced their intention to marry on _date_, and ask for your prayers."

GATHERING

Many decisions about the entrance are affected by the space in which the marriage takes place. In the congregation's worship space, a procession with instrumental music or singing appropriate to the praise of God is fitting. The procession may include a processional cross and candles, the ministers, members of the wedding party, parents and family members, and the couple. The assembly stands for the whole procession.

When the font is located near the entrance to the church, the greeting, introduction, and declaration of intention may take place at the font. A hymn of praise and an entrance procession may follow, and then the prayer of the day.

During the declaration of intention, parents may stand behind their children and place a hand on the shoulders of their children while responding to the question addressed to families. Parents or others may speak additional words of blessing and encouragement at this time or after the nuptial blessing.

When those to be married are bringing children into this new family, declarations of intention may include questions to the couple as parents and possibly to the children (see the example at declaration of intention C). Careful pastoral discretion is needed to ensure the appropriateness of these or similar questions in a given situation and to avoid any manipulation of children who are not of an age to answer for themselves.

WORD

Scripture readings may be proclaimed by family members, members of the wedding party, or others who read with confidence. When holy communion is celebrated, the last reading is from the gospels and is normally proclaimed by the presiding minister, and the assembly stands for this reading.

Vocal and instrumental music may be interspersed with the readings: in particular, a psalm may be sung in response to a reading from the Old Testament, an acclamation may be sung to welcome the gospel, and a hymn of the day may follow the sermon.

MARRIAGE

In addition to the examples of vows presented here, other forms, such as vows prepared by those to be married, will include the promise of lifelong commitment and an expression of the complete sharing that marriage implies.

When rings are given, two rings are normally used. When only one ring is used, the prayer before the giving of the ring is modified accordingly.

In places where the form of acclamation (announcement) of marriage by the presiding minister is prescribed by law, that form should be used instead.

In addition to spoken and sung acclamations by the assembly, the assembly may acclaim the newly married couple with applause.

Other visible symbols or symbolic actions may underscore the spoken vows of marriage. For example, several African and African American traditions include the symbolic gestures of jumping over a broom or enfolding the couple with a length of kente cloth.

PRAYER

The presiding minister may extend a hand over the couple while praying the nuptial blessing. A prayer for the gift of children may be added as appropriate (see nuptial blessing B).

The couple and the assembly stand for the intercessory prayers. Intercessory prayers are crafted or adapted for the local context. The prayers in the rite may serve as a starting point for developing these prayers. When communion is not celebrated, the Lord's Prayer concludes the prayers.

MEAL

The marriage liturgy is presented here within the context of holy communion. This sacrament is celebrated with the whole assembly and is not limited to the couple or the wedding party. If circumstances prevent including the assembly in the eucharistic meal, the marriage liturgy without communion is used.

Assisting ministers may be members of the families or members of the wedding party. The newly married couple may serve as ministers of communion.

SENDING

The assembly stands for the sending. When communion is not celebrated, the greeting of peace may precede the blessing and dismissal. The newly married may exchange the peace with one another and with the ministers, and all in the assembly may greet one another with the peace of Christ.

Healing

Shape of the Rite

The church embraces the ministry of healing as an important way of bringing the loving care of God to people in their need. Although the dimensions of this healing work are many and include a variety of institutions dedicated to it, the ministry of healing has its foundation in the prayer of the worshiping community, whether in the Sunday assembly or where two or three are gathered at a particular time of need.

The church's ministry of healing emphasizes caring for the sick in the widest possible understanding of that term. Every human person stands in need of healing in some dimension of life. Healing is a gift that need not be limited to those seeking remedy from a specific injury or illness. The Christian assembly at worship may embrace the gift of healing as it applies to various needs—for example, physical, emotional, spiritual, relational—that may be present among those gathered. Finally, the church's ministry of healing extends also to those nearing the end of life, as it lifts up in prayer all human decision-making and entrusts the dying into the gracious arms of God.

The liturgical ministry of healing is grounded in the life, death, and resurrection of Jesus Christ, the Word of God, whose presence we experience tangibly in baptism and the eucharist. In addition to these means of grace in word and sacrament, the ministry of healing has long included the prayer of faith, words of forgiveness and encouragement, and gestures such as the touch of a hand and anointing with oil.

In the rite of healing, the church does not replace the gifts of God that come through the scientific community nor does it promise a cure. Rather, the church offers and celebrates gifts such as these: God's presence with strength and comfort in time of suffering, God's promise of wholeness and peace, and God's love embodied in the community of faith.

GATHERING

Within the primary weekly assembly, or at other times set aside for corporate liturgies of healing, the assembly may gather as is customary. In homes, hospitals, and other similar settings, the gathering may include a greeting that affirms the connection between a person and the community from which he or she may be separated due to illness.

WORD

Many of the readings in the lectionary proclaim themes and stories of healing. Sundays that include these themes may be especially fitting times to include a rite of healing. At other times, scriptures may be selected from the list appended to this rite, or from other sources. The hymn of the day following the readings and sermon is another occasion to proclaim the gift of healing.

HEALING
Introduction
Litany for Healing
Blessing of Oil
Laying On of Hands
Anointing with Oil

Within the assembly, a pastoral introduction to the healing rite is an opportunity to articulate the church's practice of healing with those who are gathered. In smaller gatherings, the introduction may speak more directly to the particular needs of one who is ill. The litany or intercessory prayers raise up particular circumstances in which healing is sought, within the context of the needs of the whole world for reconciliation and restoration.

The practice of the laying on of hands has deep roots in the apostolic tradition as part of the healing ministry. The laying on of hands describes a ritual act in which the hands of a minister of the church are carefully placed, usually on the head of the sufferer, as prayer is offered. In the present cultural context, the intimacy of touch and its potential for misuse have led to an ambivalence about the act of touching for many people. In a countercultural way, the church maintains this ritual gesture and exercises great care in its use.

The use of oil in the church's ministry of healing is commended already in the New Testament (James 5:14). Anointing the forehead with oil is a powerful remembrance of the anointing of baptism, proclaiming that the baptized is united with Christ the Anointed One and marked with the cross of Christ forever. The oil of anointing (olive oil is customarily used) also has long association with healing because of the ancient use of oil as a salve to alleviate suffering.

[MEAL]

In the eucharist the people of God give thanks for life and wholeness, salvation and resurrection, even as they are united as the body of Christ in the bread of life and cup of blessing. Whether celebrated in the assembly or extended to those in special circumstances, the holy meal is a healing gift of God that is fittingly a part of the liturgy of healing.

SENDING
Sending Prayer
Blessing
Dismissal

In the sending rite of the community gathered for worship, or as a conclusion for a smaller gathering, the sending prayer and blessing may once more reinforce the themes of healing and the blessing of God.

HEALING

Outline

GATHERING

WORD

HEALING
Introduction
Litany for Healing
Blessing of Oil
Laying On of Hands
Anointing with Oil

[MEAL]

SENDING
Blessing
Dismissal

LITURGY of HEALING

GATHERING

When this rite is used in the corporate worship of the assembly, the gathering may include confession and forgiveness, music and song, a greeting by the presiding minister, and the prayer of the day.

When this rite is used with an individual or small group in a hospital or home, the minister may bring greetings from the community of faith in these or similar words:
Peace to you from our Lord Jesus Christ.
Your sisters and brothers in faith at *name of congregation or community*
send their love and remember you in their prayers.
The prayer of the day may follow.

WORD

Suggested readings are listed on pages 32–33. Two or three readings are proclaimed. When communion is celebrated, the last is a reading from the gospels. A psalm may be sung or said in response to a reading from the Old Testament. A sung acclamation may precede the reading of the gospel. The sermon and hymn of the day follow.

When the healing rite is included in the Sunday assembly, the propers for the day are used, followed by the sermon and hymn of the day.

In a hospital or home, a single reading, or a psalm and a reading, may be used, followed by conversation as desired.

HEALING

INTRODUCTION

The presiding minister may address the assembly in these or similar words:
Our Lord Jesus healed many who were sick as a sign of the reign of God come near, and sent the disciples to continue this work of healing. Through prayer in Jesus' name, and by the laying on of hands and anointing, the disciples witnessed to the power and presence of God. In the name of Christ, the great healer and reconciler of the world, we now entrust to God all who are in need of healing and hope. We offer our prayers for those who are gathered here, and especially for *name/s*. We commend them to the grace of Jesus Christ, that God may ease their suffering and grant them health and salvation.

LITANY FOR HEALING

A litany or another form of prayer is offered. Prepared or adapted for the particular occasion, the prayer may include the following or similar petitions. An assisting minister may lead the prayer:

A pp. 34–36 ▸

Let us pray for all who are in need of healing and hope.

Loving God, our source and our final home,
we give you thanks for the gifts of life on earth
and of new life in baptism.
In your great mercy,
hear us, O God.

Merciful God, by the wounds of your Son we are healed.
Bring health and hope to all your people.
In your great mercy,
hear us, O God.

Holy God, your Spirit came over the waters of baptism
and brought us into the communion of saints.
Renew in us the grace of baptism,
by which we share in Christ's death and resurrection.
In your great mercy,
hear us, O God.

Mighty God, whose Son brought healing and wholeness to all,
bring your healing presence now to all who are sick or in pain,
and to all who have lost hope.
In your great mercy,
hear us, O God.

Gentle God, your Son called little children to himself.
Help all children who are sick or disabled,
take them in your loving arms,
and nourish them with your grace.
In your great mercy,
hear us, O God.

Compassionate God, the strength of those who suffer,
bring hope and peace to all who are in mental, physical, or spiritual distress.
In your great mercy,
hear us, O God.

Almighty God, source of human knowledge,
give skill, wisdom, and compassion
to all who provide medical care.
In your great mercy,
hear us, O God.

Loving God, our creator and redeemer,
give gentleness and hope
to family members, friends, and caregivers of those who suffer.
In your great mercy,
hear us, O God.

Other petitions may be offered. The presiding minister concludes the prayers:
God of great and abundant mercy,
with your presence sustain *name/s*
and all whom we name before you.
Drive away their suffering, give them firm hope,
and strengthen their trust in you; through Jesus Christ our Lord.
Amen.

BLESSING OF OIL

The presiding minister may pray the following or a similar prayer:
A
We give you thanks, O God, source of life and health,
for in Jesus you became flesh
and came to know the depth of human suffering.
You sent the disciples to heal those who were sick.
Bless this oil, that all who are anointed with it
may be healed, strengthened, and renewed
by the power of your Holy Spirit.
Amen.

pp. 36–37 ▶

LAYING ON OF HANDS and ANOINTING

The presiding minister may address the assembly in these or similar words:
The ministry of Jesus invites us to new life in God and with each other. In the laying on of hands (and anointing), we proclaim the good news that God desires us to be healthy and one in the body of Christ. You are invited to offer yourself, whatever your sickness of spirit, mind, or body, and receive a sign of healing and wholeness in the name of the triune God.

During this time, hymns, psalms, and other acclamations may be sung (see p. 37). Those who wish to receive laying on of hands (and anointing) approach and, as conditions permit, they may kneel. The minister lays both hands on each person's head and following a brief silence says:

A

Name,
in the name of our Savior Jesus Christ,
may you be strengthened
and filled with God's grace,
that you may know
the healing power of the Spirit.
Response: Amen.

B

Name, in the name of God
the holy and undivided Trinity,
may Christ be present with you,
to comfort you,
to guard and protect you,
and to keep you in everlasting life.
Response: Amen.

The minister may also anoint the person's forehead with oil, making the sign of the cross and saying:

A

Receive this oil ✛ as a sign
of forgiveness and healing
in Jesus Christ.
Response: Amen.

B

p. 37 ▶

Almighty God bless you
with the healing power of the Holy Spirit,
release you from suffering,
and restore you to wholeness.
through ✛ Jesus Christ our Lord.
Response: Amen.

After all have returned to their places, the presiding minister continues:
Let us pray.

A

God of mercy, source of all healing,
we give you thanks
for your gifts of strength and life,
and especially for the gift
of your Son, Jesus Christ,
the health and salvation of the world.
Help us by your Holy Spirit
to feel your power in our lives
and to know your eternal love;
through Jesus Christ our Lord.
Amen.

B

Living God,
through this holy anointing
grant our *sisters and brothers*
comfort in *their* suffering.
When *they* are afraid, give *them* courage,
when afflicted, give *them* patience,
when dejected, afford *them* hope,
and when alone, assure *them*
of the support of your holy people.
We ask this through Christ our Lord.
Amen.

When the rite does not include holy communion, the liturgy may conclude with the Lord's Prayer, blessing, and dismissal.

MEAL

Within the corporate worship of the assembly, the liturgy continues with the greeting of peace and the remainder of the liturgy of the meal.

In a hospital or home, appropriate material from rites for distribution or celebration of communion with those in special circumstances may be used.

After the communion, an assisting minister may lead the following or a similar prayer:

PRAYER AFTER COMMUNION

A
p. 38 ►

Generous God, you sent your Son to be the bread of life,
and you give us also the cup of blessing.
We give you thanks and praise for this sacrament of healing.
Strengthen us by the power of this gift of heavenly food,
that we may all be healed
and be filled with faith and hope in your Son,
Jesus Christ our Lord.
Amen.

SENDING

BLESSING

The presiding minister blesses the assembly:
A
p. 38 ►

May the God of all consolation bless you in every way
and grant you hope all the days of your life.
May God restore you to health and grant you salvation.
May God fill your heart with peace and lead you to eternal life.
Almighty God bless you,
the Father, the ☩ Son, and the Holy Spirit.
Amen.

DISMISSAL

An assisting minister may send the assembly forth:
Go in peace. Serve the Lord.
Thanks be to God.

Scripture Readings

OLD TESTAMENT

Exodus 16:13-15	*Manna in the wilderness*	Proper 20A, Proper 13B
1 Kings 17:17-24	*Elijah restores the widow's son to life*	Proper 5C
2 Kings 5:9-14	*Healing of Naaman*	Epiphany 6B
Isaiah 11:1-3a	*The gifts of the Spirit*	Advent 2A
Isaiah 35:1-10	*The promise of God's coming*	Advent 3A, Proper 13B, St. Luke
Isaiah 42:1-7	*The suffering servant*	Epiphany 1A, Monday in Holy Week ABC
Isaiah 53:3-5	*With his stripes we are healed*	Proper 11A, Good Friday ABC
Isaiah 61:1-3	*Good tidings to the afflicted*	Advent 3B
Jeremiah 29:10-14	*God's comforting presence in an unknown future*	
Ezekiel 36:26-28	*A new heart I will give you*	Vigil of Easter ABC

PSALM

Psalm 13	*My heart is joyful because of your saving help*	Proper 8A
Psalm 20:1-6	*May the Lord answer you in the day of trouble*	Proper 6B
Psalm 23	*You anoint my head with oil*	Lent 4A, Easter 4A, Proper 23A, Proper 11B
Psalm 27	*The Lord is the strength of my life*	Epiphany 3A, Lent 2C
Psalm 91	*God shall give the angels charge over you*	Lent 1C, Proper 24B
Psalm 103	*God forgives you all your sins*	Proper 3B, St. Michael and All Angels
Psalm 121	*Our help is in the name of the Lord*	Lent 2A, Proper 24C
Psalm 130	*My soul waits for the Lord*	Lent 5A, Vigil of Pentecost ABC, Proper 5B
Psalm 138	*You will make good your purpose*	Epiphany 5C, Proper 16A, Proper 12C
Psalm 139	*Where can I go from your Spirit?*	Epiphany 2B
Psalm 145	*The eyes of all wait upon you*	Proper 9A, Proper 13A, Proper 12B

NEW TESTAMENT

Acts 3:1-10	*Peter and John heal the lame man*	
Acts 5:12-16	*Healings in Jerusalem*	
Acts 10:36-43	*Apostolic preaching*	Epiphany 1ABC, Easter Day ABC
Acts 16:16-18	*The slave girl with the spirit of divination*	Easter 7C
Romans 8:18-23	*We await the redemption of our bodies*	Proper 11A
Romans 8:31-39	*Nothing can separate us from the love of God*	Proper 12A
2 Corinthians 1:3-5	*God comforts us in affliction*	
Hebrews 12:1-2	*Jesus, the perfecter of our faith*	Wednesday in Holy Week ABC
James 5:13-16	*Is any among you sick? Prayer of faith*	
1 John 5:13-15	*Faith conquers the world*	

GOSPEL

Matthew 5:2-10	*The beatitudes*	Epiphany 4A, All Saints Sunday A
Matthew 8:1-8,13-17	*Jesus healed many*	
Matthew 26: 36-39	*Jesus' prayer in the garden*	Lent 6A
Mark 1:21-28	*Healing of the man with the unclean spirit*	Epiphany 4B
Mark 1:29-34a	*Healing of Peter's mother-in-law and others*	Epiphany 5B
Mark 5:1-20	*Healing of Gerasene man possessed by a demon*	
Mark 5:22-24	*Request for healing over Jairus' daughter*	Proper 8B
Mark 6:7, 12-13	*They anointed many with oil who were sick*	Proper 9B
Luke 17:11-19	*Your faith has made you well*	Proper 23C, Day of Thanksgiving A
John 5:1b-9	*Do you want to be healed?*	Easter 6C
John 6:47-51	*I am the bread of life*	Proper 14B
John 9:1-11	*Healing of the man born blind*	Lent 4A

Supplemental Materials

LITANY FOR HEALING

B

To the triune God, the source of all love and all life, let us offer our prayers.

God, our creator,
your will for us and for all your people is health and salvation:
Lord of life,
hear our prayer.

Jesus Christ, Son of God,
you came that we might have life and have it in abundance:
Lord of life,
hear our prayer.

Holy Spirit, dwelling within us,
you make us temples of your presence:
Lord of life,
hear our prayer.

For all who are in need of healing:
silence
Lord of life,
hear our prayer.

For all who are suffering from injury or illness:
silence
Lord of life,
hear our prayer.

For all who are troubled by confusion or pain:
silence
Lord of life,
hear our prayer.

For all whose increasing years bring weariness:
silence
Lord of life,
hear our prayer.

For all about to undergo surgery:
silence
Lord of life,
hear our prayer.

For all who cannot sleep:
silence
Lord of life,
hear our prayer.

For all who practice the healing arts:
silence
Lord of life,
hear our prayer.

Other petitions may be offered. The presiding minister concludes the prayers:
Compassionate God, you so loved the world
that you sent us Jesus to bear our infirmities and afflictions.
Through acts of healing, he revealed you as the true source of health and salvation.
For the sake of your Christ who suffered and died for us,
conquered death, and now reigns with you in glory,
hear the cry of your people.
Have mercy on us, make us whole,
and bring us at last into the fullness of your eternal life.
Amen.

C
This form is suitable for the Sunday assembly, incorporating the intercessory prayers.

Let us pray for the whole people of God in Christ Jesus,
and especially for all those here and around the world
who are suffering or are in any affliction.

Merciful God, you sent your Son to be our peace.
Help all those who suffer any pain or grief, hopelessness or anxiety.
God of mercy,
hear our prayer.

Mighty God, the strength of the weak and the comfort of those who suffer,
mercifully grant to *name/s* the help of your presence,
that their sickness and pain may be turned into health.
God of mercy,
hear our prayer.

God of peace and reconciliation,
bring an end to the sickness of the world,
especially violence, terrorism, war, and their causes.
God of mercy,
hear our prayer.

Holy God, Holy One, your Son prayed that your people may be one.
May the gift of baptism be a power for healing the church's brokenness,
and bless all efforts for renewal and Christian unity.
God of mercy,
hear our prayer.

Loving God, mend broken relationships and bring peace
to our families, our congregation, this community, and the world.
God of mercy,
hear our prayer.

Other petitions may be offered.

Eternal God, we thank you for all the faithful departed, (especially *name/s,*)
and those whom we remember before you. . . .
Heal the pain of all who grieve.
God of mercy,
hear our prayer.

The presiding minister concludes the prayers:
O God, we bring these intercessions before you,
knowing that you will hear us as you have promised,
and will answer according to the mercy shown in your Son,
Jesus Christ our Lord.
Amen.

BLESSING OF OIL

B

Gracious God, source of all healing,
in Jesus Christ you heal the sick and mend the broken.
We bless you for this oil pressed from the fruits of the earth,
given to us as a sign of healing and forgiveness, and of the fullness of life you give.
By your Spirit, come upon all who are anointed with this oil
that they may receive your healing touch and be made whole,
to the glory of Jesus Christ our redeemer.
Amen.

C

Sun of righteousness, you bring healing light
to all who are shadowed by grief and suffering.
We give you thanks for the gift of oil,
a sign of grace and favor for your people throughout the ages.
In baptism you anoint us and call us your own.
Send your Holy Spirit on us and on this healing balm,
that through this anointing your people may look to you
as the source of health and salvation;
through Jesus Christ our Savior.
Amen.

ACCLAMATION

A

Healer of boundless compassion,
peace for our suffering hearts:
Anoint us with health,
embrace us with strength,
and bring us to fullness of life.

B

May the God of all healing
enfold us in love,
fill us with peace,
and lead us to wholeness and strength.

C

Blessed be God,
who forgives all our sins,
who heals all our ills,
who crowns us with mercy and love.

ANOINTING WITH OIL

C

Almighty God deliver you from all evil,
preserve you in all goodness,
and bring you to everlasting life,
through ✠ Jesus Christ our Lord.

PRAYER AFTER COMMUNION

B

Merciful God, constant source of all healing,
we give you thanks for all your gifts of strength and life,
and above all we thank you for the gift of your Son,
through whom we have health and salvation.
As we wait for that day when there will be no more pain,
help us by your Holy Spirit to be assured of your power in our lives
and to trust in your eternal love; through Jesus Christ our Lord.
Amen.

BLESSING

B

May God who goes before you through desert places by night and by day
be your companion and guide;
may your journey be with the saints;
may the Holy Spirit be your strength, and Christ your clothing of light,
both now and forever.
Amen.

OTHER PRAYERS

One or more of these prayers may be used in various circumstances.

A (general)

Almighty God, giver of life and health: Send your blessing on all who are sick, and upon those who minister to them, that all weakness may be vanquished by the triumph of the risen Christ; who lives and reigns forever and ever.

B (for those who suffer)

Merciful Lord, you sent your Son to be our peace. Help all who suffer pain or grief to find in Christ strength and peace, so that their trust in your promises may be renewed; through Jesus Christ our Lord.

C (for those in affliction)

Almighty and everlasting God, comfort of the sad and strength to those who suffer:
Let the prayers of your children who are in any trouble rise to you. To everyone in distress, grant mercy, grant relief, grant refreshment, through Jesus Christ our Lord.

D (for recovery from sickness)

O God, the strength of the weak and the comfort of sufferers, mercifully hear our prayers and grant to your *servant/s name/s* the help of your power, that *their* sickness may be turned into health and our sorrow into joy, through Jesus Christ our Lord.

E (for those who minister in healing)

Almighty God, source of human knowledge and skill: Guide physicians and nurses and all those you have called to practice the arts of healing. Strengthen them by your life-giving Spirit, that, by their ministries, the health of all people may be promoted and your creation may be glorified; through Jesus Christ our Lord.

F (for the ministry of family and friends)

Loving God, our creator and redeemer, give strength and gentleness, patience and faithfulness to family members and friends. Let their hope be in you, and by their ministry of love, let your love be known; through Jesus Christ our Lord.

G (for those who desire the prayer of the church)

Blessed Lord, we ask your loving care and protection for those who are sick in body, mind, or spirit and who desire our prayers. Take from them all fears and help them to put their trust in you, that they may feel your strong arms around them. Touch them with your renewing love, that they may know wholeness in you and glorify your name; through Jesus Christ our Lord.

H (for those making decisions)

O Lord our God, send your Holy Spirit to guide us, that we may make our decisions with love, mercy, and reverence for your gift of life; through your Son, Jesus Christ our Lord.

I (for strength and confidence)

Holy God, giver of life and health, comfort and relieve your servant _name_, and give your power of healing to those who minister to *her/his* needs, that *she/he* may be strengthened in weakness and have confidence in your loving care, through Jesus Christ our Lord.

J (for a sick child)

Lord Jesus Christ, Good Shepherd of the sheep, you gather the lambs in your arms and carry them in safety. We commend to your loving care this child _name_. Relieve *her/his* pain, guard *her/him* from all danger, restore to *her/him* your gifts of gladness and strength, and raise *her/him* up to a life of service to you. Hear us, we pray, for your dear name's sake.

K (before surgery or treatment)

Almighty God, graciously comfort _name_ in *her/his* suffering, and bless the means that are used for relief and for healing. Fill *her/his* heart with confidence that, though at times *she/he* may be afraid, *she/he* may yet put *her/his* trust in you, through Jesus Christ our Lord.

L (before surgery or treatment)

Strengthen your servant _name_, O God, to do what *she/h*e must do and bear what *she/he* must bear; that, accepting your healing gifts through the skill of the medical staff, *she/he* may be restored to health; through Jesus Christ our Lord.

M (thanksgiving for a beginning of recovery)

O Lord, your compassions never fail and your mercies are new every morning. We give you thanks for giving our *sister/brother name* both relief from pain and hope of health renewed. Continue in *her/him* the good work you have begun; that *she/he,* daily increasing in bodily strength and rejoicing in your goodness, may so order *her/his* life and conduct that *she/he* may always think and do those things that please you; through Jesus Christ our Lord.

COMMENDATION of the DYING

When a person is near death, the pastor should be notified, so that the ministry of the church may be provided. A person approaching death may be offered the opportunity for confession and forgiveness.

The following rite may be shortened or extended as appropriate, and may be led by an ordained minister or another leader. The prayers may be adapted as needed.

GATHERING

The leader greets those present with one or both of the following, or in similar words:

A
We come together for prayer
to commend *name* to God,
who is faithful and compassionate.

B
We begin in the name
in which we are baptized,
in the name of the Father,
and of the ✝ Son, and of the Holy Spirit.

Let us pray.

A   *p. 44* ▶
Almighty God, look on *name,* whom you made your child in baptism.
Comfort *her/him* with the promise of life with all your saints,
the promise made sure by the death and resurrection
of your Son, Jesus Christ our Lord.
Amen.

WORD

PSALM

One of the following or another psalm may be said:
Psalm 23   *The Lord is my shepherd*
Psalm 61:1-5   *Hear my cry, O God*
Psalm 130   *Out of the depths, I cry to you, O Lord*
Psalm 139:1-12   *O Lord, you have searched me and known me*

LITANY

The leader invites those present into prayer, using these or similar words:

Let us offer our prayers for *name,*
saying, We commend *name* to you.

Holy God, creator of heaven and earth,
we commend *name* to you.
Holy and Mighty, redeemer of the world,
we commend *name* to you.
Holy and Immortal, sanctifier of the faithful,
we commend *name* to you.
Holy, blessed, and glorious Trinity, one God,
we commend *name* to you.

By your holy incarnation,
we commend *name* to you.
By your cross and passion,
we commend *name* to you.
By your precious death and burial,
we commend *name* to you.
By your glorious resurrection and ascension,
we commend *name* to you.
By the coming of the Holy Spirit,
we commend *name* to you.

For deliverance from all evil, all sin, and all tribulation,
we commend *name* to you.
For deliverance from eternal death,
we commend *name* to you.
For forgiveness of all sins,
we commend *name* to you.
For a place of refreshment at your heavenly banquet,
we commend *name* to you.
For joy and gladness with your saints in light,
we commend *name* to you.

Jesus, Lamb of God,
we commend *name* to you.
Jesus, bearer of our sins,
we commend *name* to you.
Jesus, redeemer of the world,
we commend *name* to you.

The Lord's Prayer follows. Appropriate portions of additional rites may also be included: the laying on of hands and anointing with oil from the Liturgy of Healing; the celebration or distribution of communion with those in special circumstances.

COMMENDATION

The leader continues:
Let us commend our *sister/brother* <u>name</u> to the mercy of God, our maker and redeemer.

The leader and others who are present may lay a hand on the head of the dying person as the leader says one or more of the following:

A p. 44 ▶

Lord Jesus Christ,
deliver your servant <u>name</u> from all evil
and set *her/him* free from every bond,
that *she/he* may join all your saints
in the eternal courts of heaven,
where with the Father and the Holy Spirit
you live and reign, one God,
now and forever.
Amen.

B
<u>Name,</u> our *sister/brother* in the faith,
we entrust you to God who created you.
May you return to the one who formed us out of the dust of the earth.
Surrounded by the angels and triumphant saints,
may Christ come to meet you as you go forth from this life.
Christ, the Lord of glory, who was crucified for you,
bring you freedom and peace.
Christ, the High Priest, who has forgiven all your sins,
keep you among his people.
Christ, the Son of God, who died for you,
show you the glories of his eternal kingdom.
Christ, the Good Shepherd, enfold you with his tender care.
May you see your redeemer face to face and enjoy the sight of God forever.
Amen.

The leader may continue, particularly when death seems near:
Into your hands, O merciful Savior, we commend your servant <u>name</u>.
Acknowledge, we humbly beseech you,
a sheep of your own fold, a lamb of your flock, a sinner of your own redeeming.
Receive *her/him* into the arms of your mercy,
into the blessed rest of everlasting peace,
and into the glorious company of the saints in light.
Amen.

After death, the leader may say:
Lord Jesus Christ,
through water and the Spirit you brought *name* into your family;
receive *her/him* and present *her/him* to God Most High.
Amen.

O Lord, support us all the day long of this troubled life,
until the shadows lengthen and the evening comes and the busy world is hushed,
the fever of life is over, and our work is done.
Then, Lord, in your mercy, grant us a safe lodging, and a holy rest, and peace at the last;
through Jesus Christ our Lord.
Amen.

*Prayers may be included for the family and other bereaved. Those present may be invited to offer
prayers. Then the leader says one or both of the following:*

A	B
May *name* and all the faithful departed,	Almighty God, Father, ✛ Son,
through the mercy of God, rest in peace.	and Holy Spirit, bless us now and forever.
Amen.	**Amen.**

Supplemental Materials

PRAYER AT THE GATHERING

B

Merciful God, as your servant Mary stood at the foot of the cross,
we stand before you with broken hearts and tear-filled eyes.
Keep us mindful that you know our pain,
and lead us to see your resurrection power already at work in *name*.
In your time, raise us from our grief
even as you promise to raise *name* to life eternal;
through Jesus Christ our Savior.
Amen.

C (for a child who is dying)

God our creator, you called into being this fragile life,
which had seemed to us so full of promise.
Give to *name*, whom we commit to your care, abundant life in your presence,
and to us who grieve, courage to bear our loss;
through Jesus Christ our Savior.
Amen.

COMMENDATION

C

Name, our companion in faith and *sister/brother* in Christ, we entrust you to God.
Go forth from this world in the love of God who created you;
in the mercy of Jesus Christ who died for you;
in the power of the Holy Spirit who strengthens you,
at one with all the faithful, living and departed.
May you rest in peace and rise in the glory of your eternal home,
where grief and misery are banished, and light and joy abide.
Amen.

D

Name, child of God, go forth in the name of God the Father Almighty who created you;
in the name of Jesus Christ, Son of the living God, who redeemed you;
in the name of the Holy Spirit who was poured out upon you.
May you rest in peace and dwell forever in the paradise of God.
Amen.

PRAYER WHEN LIFE-SUSTAINING CARE ENDS

This rite is appropriate when a person gathers with others (family, friends, caregivers) for prayer to mark a transition from life-sustaining to palliative care. It may also be used when extraordinary measures are to be withheld or discontinued.

The rite is for situations in which death is expected to follow not long after the withholding or discontinuing of treatment. When death is expected immediately following, the rite for the Commendation of the Dying might be preferred.

The service may be abbreviated or lengthened as needed.

GATHERING

The leader greets those present and invites them into prayer.

We gather to entrust *name* to the care of God,
who alone is our life,
whose steadfast love endures forever.

Let us pray.

A

O God our creator and sustainer,
receive our prayers for *name*.
We thank you
for the love and companionship
we have shared with *her/him*.
Give us grace now to accept
the limits of human healing
as we commend *name* to your merciful care.
Strengthen us, we pray, in this time of trial
and help us to continue
to serve and care for one another;
through Jesus Christ our Savior.
Amen.

B

Lord of all wisdom and source of all life,
we come before you as we struggle
with decisions about life and death
that rightly belong to you alone.
Name lies in grave illness.
We confess to you
that we act with uncertainty now.
Give us your help and guide us, O God,
in your loving concern for *name*;
through Jesus Christ our Redeemer.
Amen.

WORD

One or more of the following passages of scripture may be read:

OLD TESTAMENT

Isaiah 49:14-16a	*I will not forget you*
Isaiah 65:17-20	*I am about to create a new heaven and a new earth*

PSALM

Psalm 23	*The Lord is my shepherd*
Psalm 103:8-13	*The Lord is merciful and gracious*

NEW TESTAMENT

Romans 6:3-4, 8-11	*Death no longer has dominion*
Romans 8:35, 37-39	*Who will separate us from the love of Christ*

GOSPEL

Matthew 11:28-30	*I will give you rest*
John 14:1-3	*In my Father's house*

PRAYER

A litany is prayed, introduced by the leader. Silence may follow each response:

A   p. 48 ▶

Let us pray to God, our refuge and strength,
saying, help us, O God.

That we may know your near presence with us:
help us, O God.
That *name* may be released from the bonds of suffering:
help us, O God.
That our actions may proceed from love:
help us, O God.
That our best judgments may accord with your will:
help us, O God.
That you will hold *name* and us in the palm of your hand this day:
help us, O God.
That all our fears may be relieved as we place our trust in you:
help us, O God.
That although we grieve now, joy and peace may be restored:
help us, O God.

The leader concludes the litany with these or similar words:
God our wisdom, bless the decisions we have made in hope, in sorrow, and in love,
that as we place our whole trust in you,
our choices and our actions may be encompassed by your grace;
through Jesus Christ who died and rose for us.
Amen.

The Lord's Prayer follows. Appropriate portions of additional rites may also be included: the laying on of hands and anointing with oil from the Liturgy of Healing; the celebration or distribution of communion with those in special circumstances.

SENDING

PRAYER OF COMMITMENT

The leader may offer this or a similar prayer:
Let us pray that we may be a sign of Christ's presence with *name* in life and in death.

Faithful God, give comfort and strength to *name*
as *she/he* follows Christ in the path that is now set before *her/him*.
Give wisdom and faithfulness to all of us who are companions along this way,
that we may journey beside our loved one,
watch and wait with *her/him*,
and, with your help, bear witness by our presence and prayers
to the love of Jesus Christ, your Son, our Savior.
Amen.

GREETING OF PEACE

If the peace has not been shared as part of holy communion, all present may greet one another in the name of Christ. Those present may touch the hand or forehead of the dying person and say, Peace be with you.

BLESSING

Glory to God whose power, working in us,
can do infinitely more than we can ask or imagine;
glory to God from generation to generation in the church
and in Christ Jesus forever and ever.
Amen.

After this, life-sustaining treatment may be ended in accordance with the circumstances.

Commendation of the Dying may follow at a time when death is imminent.

Supplemental Materials

LITANY

B

With the faithful of every time and place, let us place ourselves in God's hands, saying, God of the promise, we put our trust in you.

With Sarah and Abraham, who set out from home for a land unknown:
God of the promise,
we put our trust in you.
With Moses, who prayed for his people before going up the mountain to die:
God of the promise,
we put our trust in you.
With Ruth, who pledged faithfulness until death to her mother-in-law Naomi:
God of the promise,
we put our trust in you.
With the three young men, who walked through the fiery furnace and were delivered:
God of the promise,
we put our trust in you.
With the magi, who followed the star to the child in Bethlehem:
God of the promise,
we put our trust in you.
With the disciples, who left their nets to follow Jesus:
God of the promise,
we put our trust in you.
With Mary the mother of Jesus and the women who watched at the cross:
God of the promise,
we put our trust in you.
With our Lord Jesus, who commended himself into your hands when he breathed his last:
God of the promise,
we put our trust in you.
With *name*, whom we now place into your strong arms, confident of your grace and mercy:
God of the promise,
we put our trust in you.

OTHER PRAYERS

A (for health care providers)

God, our healer and redeemer, we give thanks for the compassionate care *name* has received. Bless *name/s of those present, or others* and all caregivers. Give them knowledge, virtue, and patience; strengthen them for their ministry of comfort and healing; through Jesus Christ our Savior.

B (for all who suffer)

O God, look with mercy on all those who suffer, and heal their spirits, that they may be delivered from sickness and fear. Restore hope for the desolate, give rest to the weary, comfort the sorrowful, be with the dying; and bring them, finally, to their true heavenly home, for Jesus Christ's sake.

C (for one whose treatment is to be withheld or discontinued)

Holy God, whose peace passes all understanding, we pray that in your good time you will free *name* from all earthly cares, pardon *her/his* sins, release *her/him* from pain, and grant that *she/he* may come to dwell with all your saints in everlasting glory, for the sake of Jesus Christ.

D (for guidance)

Lord God, you have called your servants to ventures of which we cannot see the ending, by paths as yet untrodden, through perils unknown. Give us faith to go out with good courage, not knowing where we go, but only that your hand is leading us and your love supporting us; through Jesus Christ our Lord.

CONFESSION and FORGIVENESS
Individual Order

Confession and forgiveness with a penitent individual is a part of the church's ministry of healing in its broadest sense. One aspect of sin is the brokenness of relationships intended by God to be life-giving: relationships with God, the neighbor, the creation, and the self. Confession and forgiveness is the beginning of the healing of broken relationships, a step on the way to reconciliation and wholeness.

This order for confession and forgiveness may be used by itself, at times when a congregation offers the opportunity or persons request the opportunity for confession; it may also be used in conjunction with pastoral counseling, such as to conclude a counseling session. Where appropriate, this order or a corporate form of confession and forgiveness may also be used in association with rites of healing and commendation of the dying.

The confession made by a penitent is protected from disclosure. A pastor is obligated to respect at all times the confidential nature of the confession.

INVITATION

The pastor invites the penitent to the prayer of confession with these or similar words:
If we confess our sins,
God who is faithful and just will forgive us our sins
and cleanse us from all unrighteousness.
God be in your heart and on your lips as you confess your sins.

PRAYER OF CONFESSION

The penitent may use the following form or make confession in her/his own words:
Merciful God, I confess that I have sinned against you and against others.
I have sinned by my own fault in thought, word, and deed,
in things I have done and left undone.
Especially I confess that I . . .
Here the penitent may confess sins that are known and that burden her/him.
I repent of these and all my sins.
I am truly sorry, and I pray for forgiveness.
I firmly intend to amend my life, and to seek help in mending what is broken.
As I turn from sin and turn to you, I ask for strength to serve you in newness of life.

The pastor may engage the penitent in pastoral conversation in which admonition, counsel, and comfort are shared.

FORGIVENESS

Addressing the penitent, the pastor may lay both hands on the head of the penitent:

A

All things have been reconciled to God
through the life, death, and resurrection
of Jesus Christ.
God is merciful and blesses you.
As a called and ordained minister
of the church of Christ, and by his authority,
I forgive you your sins
in the name of the Father,
and of the ✝ Son,
and of the Holy Spirit.
Response: Amen.

B

God is faithful and just,
full of grace and mercy
from everlasting to everlasting.
Name, in the name of Jesus Christ
I say to you: You are forgiven.
Almighty God,
who forgives all your sins,
strengthen you in all goodness,
and by the power of the Holy Spirit
keep you in eternal life.
Response: Amen.

GREETING OF PEACE

May the peace of God, which passes all understanding,
keep your heart and your mind in Christ Jesus.
Response: Amen.

The pastor and the penitent individual may exchange a sign of peace.

Additional Prayers in Development

Prayers for use by a sick person

Trust in God
Pain
Sleep
In the morning
In the evening
A child's prayer
A sick person
Protection
One suffering from mental illness
Recovery from sickness
Strength and confidence
Sleeplessness
Rest
Sanctification of illness
Before/after an operation
Extended course of treatment
Survivors of abuse and violence
Times of personal distress
Thanksgiving for recovery
One who fears losing hope
Those who are developmentally disabled
In thanksgiving
In pain
In loss of memory
In confinement
For serenity
Thanksgiving for caregivers
Comfort in God
In desolation
After the loss of a pregnancy
Diagnosis of terminal illness
Difficult treatment choices

Prayers for those who are sick

Health of body and soul
A child
A visit with someone who is sick
Release
People with incurable diseases
Those who are unconscious
A poor prognosis
In the evening
Protection
One suffering from mental illness
Recovery from sickness
Strength and confidence
The sleepless
For rest
Sanctification of illness
Before an operation
An extended course of treatment
Survivors of abuse and violence
Times of personal distress
Thanksgiving for recovery
Those who fear losing hope
Those who are developmentally disabled

Other prayers related to healing

Caregivers and others
        who support the sick
At the limits of our power to help
Health care providers
Emergency workers
Relatives of an organ donor
The chronically ill
        and those who support them
When a pregnancy is ended
Becoming old
Hospice decision
Sobriety, anniversary of sobriety
When a marriage is ended

Notes on the Rites

Liturgy of Healing

GENERAL

The Liturgy of Healing is designed primarily for corporate, public use. However, it includes resources that may be adapted for use with an individual in the course of pastoral ministry to the sick.

When this liturgy is celebrated in the primary weekly assembly, the readings and propers for the Sunday are normally used. The list of scripture readings on pages 32–33 suggests lectionary days on which healing may be especially appropriate to include in the liturgy.

The festival of Saint Luke, Evangelist (October 18), or the Sunday nearest this day, is a fitting occasion to celebrate the ministry of healing with a service of healing.

GATHERING

In the corporate worship of the assembly, the gathering rite may take its customary shape. Because confession and forgiveness have long been associated with the ministry of healing, a brief order for confession and forgiveness may be included in the gathering rite or at another place in the service.

In the primary weekly assembly, the prayer of the day for St. Luke, Evangelist may be used following the prayer appointed for the day or week in the church year.

WORD

The list of readings on pages 32–33 may serve as a source for selecting readings when the liturgy of healing is celebrated at another time than the primary weekly assembly. When holy communion is celebrated, the last reading is from the gospels and is normally proclaimed by the presiding minister, and the assembly stands for this reading.

When choosing readings for use with an individual, care is taken that the readings are appropriate to the individual and the circumstances.

HEALING

The connection of the church's healing ministry with the sacrament of baptism is reinforced when this portion of the liturgy is led from the baptismal font. One or more stations with facilities for kneeling may be set up nearby.

When this liturgy is used with an individual, the introduction may be simplified and made more personal, and appropriate selections from the litany may be prayed.

The action of the laying on of hands is a significant physical gesture of blessing that offers another link to the sacrament of baptism. Laying both hands on the head of each person, the pastor may allow a substantial silence before speaking the words of blessing.

Traditionally, olive oil is used for anointing. In synods where the bishop presides at a blessing of oils, that oil may be used. Otherwise, within a corporate service of healing, one of the prayers in this rite for blessing of oil may be used prior to the laying on of hands.

The oil may be kept in a stock (a small metal cylinder with a securely fitting lid) containing cotton to absorb the oil and prevent spillage. Or, in the assembly, oil may be poured from a vessel into a bowl or shell, allowing for a more clearly visible sign of anointing.

When anointing is offered to those who desire it, the pastor places oil on the forehead of each person in the sign of the cross, speaking the words associated with this action. When anointing is used, the laying on of hands in silence may be followed immediately by the words and action associated with the anointing.

Silence, congregational singing, and other vocal or instrumental music may accompany the laying on of hands and anointing.

When these actions are complete, the assembly stands for the concluding prayer. The Lord's Prayer, blessing, and dismissal complete the liturgy when holy communion is not celebrated.

MEAL
The liturgy of healing is presented here within the context of holy communion. When communion is celebrated, the sacrament is celebrated with the whole assembly, beginning with the greeting of peace. When the liturgy is used with an individual, the appropriate portions of rites for the celebration or distribution of communion in special circumstances may be incorporated.

SENDING
The assembly stands for the sending. One of the alternative blessing texts may be used.

Commendation of the Dying

GENERAL
With this rite, the church commends one who is dying to the care of God and supports the person with prayer at the passage of death. This ministry at the time of death is an important aspect of the pastoral ministry of the church, and pastors desire to be notified when a person is near death so that this ministry may be extended. When the pastor is prevented from being present, another person may lead the rite. When space permits, all present may gather around the one who is dying, at least for the words of commendation.

The readings, prayers, and commendations are intended to provide resources for either a brief or extended time of prayer. An abbreviated version might include the opening prayer, a single reading, selections from the litany, the Lord's Prayer, and a commendation. When vigil is kept with the dying over an extended period of time, other readings, litanies, prayers, and commendations may be added, perhaps interspersed with the singing of hymns and psalms.

When life-sustaining measures are to be withheld or discontinued, Prayer When Life-Sustaining Care Ends or portions thereof may precede Commendation of the Dying.

Confession and Forgiveness—Individual Order

GENERAL
The individual order for confession and forgiveness is included here to illustrate the breadth of the church's ministry of healing. When, on occasion, it is used with an individual in association with other rites of healing, the relationship between forgiveness and healing must be clearly articulated to avoid implying a causative link between sin and a particular illness.

As a part of their exercise of the public ministry of the church, called and ordained pastors serve as confessors. In a church setting, the pastor may vest in an alb and a stole in the color of the season.

A congregation may establish regular times when a pastor is available to hear individual confessions.

PREPARATION
Although individual confession may take place in a variety of settings, in the worship space a place near the baptismal font or the altar may be prepared. Facilities for kneeling may be provided.

INVITATION
The words of invitation provided in the rite may conclude a brief time of greeting and introduction to the significance of confession. Or, these or similar words may be used as a transition from a preceding conversation or counseling session.

PRAYER OF CONFESSION
The prayer of confession may use the form provided or may be in the penitent's own words. If additional pastoral conversation is desired, it will usually be brief.

FORGIVENESS
Laying both hands on the head of the penitent, as at baptism, the pastor speaks the words of absolution.

Funeral

Shape of the Rite

The death of a human being is a reminder of the brevity of life on earth and of the universal, inescapable nature of life's end. In the face of death, care for the dying and those who have died is a fundamental sign of humanness, giving expression to deeply held convictions about the meaning of life. The church's most deeply held conviction is the *paschal mystery*: Christ's saving passage through death to resurrected life as the new creation, the same passage into which Christ calls the baptized to follow. God's people gather around Christ in word and sacrament every Lord's day to celebrate that passage through death to life and that call to follow. So, too, when the church gathers to mark the end of life, the paschal mystery in which the baptized live is the source of worship, the heartbeat of mutual consolation, and the hope of healing.

Comforting the Bereaved

GATHERING
WORD
PRAYER

This rite is for use at the place of death, the home of the deceased, or a funeral establishment. It is the first of three stational rites, in that each rite is typically celebrated in a different location. Together with the Funeral Liturgy and finally the Committal, the church marks the end of life and commends the deceased to God.

Funeral Liturgy

GATHERING
Introduction
Greeting
Remembrance of Baptism
Procession
Prayer of the Day
Remembrance of the Deceased

The assembly that is gathered for the funeral liturgy includes relatives and friends of the deceased together with the whole community of Christ. In the name of the triune God all are welcomed and the gift of baptism is recalled. On the day of reception into the church, the baptized was washed into Christ and clothed with his righteousness; on this last day, words and symbols of baptism underscore God's faithfulness to the baptismal promise. In prayer the assembly gives thanks for the departed sister or brother and asks for God's compassion for the days ahead.

WORD
Readings
Responses
Sermon
Hymn of the Day
Creed
Intercessions

In the proclamation of scripture readings and sermon, Christ Jesus, victor over death and source of new life, is present to the assembly. Christ the Word is the spoken assurance of God's presence in every moment of life and God's gift of comfort and hope in deepest sorrow. In silent reflection, with song and confession of faith, God's people respond to the living Word. Trusting God's baptismal promises, as in life, so now in death, the deceased and those who mourn are named before Christ in prayer. The Lord's Prayer, commendation, and sending lead to the committal when the eucharist is not celebrated.

[MEAL]

The living bread and the cup of salvation, shared in community around the familiar center of the table, is full of healing power for those who grieve. On the night before his own death, Jesus gave his disciples this holy meal; on the day of resurrection, the risen Christ brought joy to the grieving disciples at Emmaus through the breaking of the bread. This sacrament is the gracious sign of the completion of baptism, the foretaste of the heavenly banquet, and the anticipation of all the faithful reunited before God and the Lamb.

COMMENDATION
Invitation
Silent Prayer
Prayer of Commendation
Farewell

The commendation marks the reality of separation. In prayer the bereaved and the entire assembly release the one who has died, commending their companion to the mercy of God and the company of the saints in light. Confidence in God's promise may be sung or said in the words of farewell.

SENDING
Blessing
Procession

This portion of the funeral liturgy concludes with simplicity, the briefest of blessings, as an indication that the committal is yet to come. If the committal occurs at a different time, another appropriate blessing and dismissal may be used.

Committal

GATHERING
Greeting
Prayer

The peace of the risen Lord, the assurance of grace, is once again the greeting to the community of faith. Words of comfort may be shared. Then, with prayer, the place of final rest is set aside in anticipation of the coming of Christ, when all the faithful shall be raised up in joy.

WORD
Reading

By this scripture reading, the church bears witness to the bereaved, as well as to the world, that death is not the last word. The last Word is Jesus Christ, the fullness of God, the fullness of life.

COMMITTAL
Committal
Response

Trusting God as the origin and destiny of all, the community makes the final commitment of a loved one into God's hands, even as Christ handed over his life on the cross. These words may include that ancient and beloved benediction with which, since the time of Moses, the name of God has been placed on the faithful.

SENDING
Prayer
Lord's Prayer
Blessing
Dismissal

The church prays for the healing presence of God in the difficult days ahead, knowing that healing will be accomplished in and through grieving. Once again, the prayer of the Savior may be spoken with one voice. All are blessed and dismissed in the name of the Holy Trinity, the same name of baptismal promise in which all had originally gathered, and in which all the faithful live.

FUNERAL

Outline

Comforting the Bereaved	*Funeral Liturgy*	*Committal*
GATHERING	GATHERING Introduction **Greeting** Remembrance of Baptism Procession **Prayer of the Day** Remembrance of the Deceased	GATHERING Greeting **Prayer**
WORD		WORD **Reading**
PRAYER		
	WORD **Readings** Responses **Sermon** Hymn of the Day Creed **Intercessions**	COMMITTAL **Committal** Response
		SENDING Prayer Lord's Prayer **Blessing** Dismissal
	[MEAL]	
	COMMENDATION Invitation Silent Prayer **Prayer of Commendation** Farewell	
	SENDING **Blessing** Procession	

COMFORTING the BEREAVED

GATHERING

The leader greets those who are present and invites into prayer with these or similar words:
We are gathered for prayer
to begin our commendation of our *sister/brother name* to the mercy of God.
Let us pray.

A	B
Lord, have mercy.	Holy God, holy and mighty,
Christ, have mercy.	holy and immortal,
Lord, have mercy.	have mercy on us.

The leader continues with one or more of the following or another appropriate prayer:

A

Eternal God, you gave *name* a new birth in baptism
and entrusted *her/him* to us to know and to love.
As we thank you for the life we shared,
help us now to release *her/him* to your mighty keeping.
Bring us all to that day when we shall stand in your presence
with all your saints in light eternal; through Jesus Christ our Lord.
Amen.

B

Merciful Creator, your Holy Spirit intercedes for us
even when we do not know how to pray.
Send your Spirit now to comfort us in these days of need and loss,
and help us to commend *name* to your merciful care;
through Jesus Christ our Lord.
Amen.

C

Almighty God, source of all mercy and giver of comfort,
graciously tend those who mourn,
that casting all their sorrow on you,
they may know the consolation of your love;
through your Son, Jesus Christ our Lord.
Amen.

D (at the death of a child)

Holy God, your beloved Son took children into his arms and blessed them.
Help us to entrust *name* to your never-failing lovingkindness.
Comfort us as we bear the pain of *her/his* death,
and gather us all into the arms of your blessing;
through Jesus Christ our Savior.
Amen.

WORD

One or more of the following or other appropriate readings are used:

OLD TESTAMENT

Isaiah 49:13b-16a	*God will not forget you*
Isaiah 54:10	*The Lord has compassion on you*

PSALM

Psalm 121	*I lift up my eyes to the hills*
Psalm 130	*Out of the depths I cry to you, O Lord*

NEW TESTAMENT

Romans 6:3-9	*Baptized into Christ Jesus*
2 Corinthians 4:16—5:1	*Prepared for eternal glory*

GOSPEL

John 10:27-29	*My sheep hear my voice*
John 14:27	*Peace I leave with you*

The leader may offer words of comfort and, if desired, engage those who are present in mutual conversation and consolation.

PRAYER

The leader continues:
Let us pray to the Lord most merciful,
saying, Hear our prayer.

Most gracious God, our *sister/brother* <u>name</u>
was given the promise of eternal life in baptism;
give *her/him* communion with your saints forever. Lord, in your mercy,
hear our prayer.

Merciful God, your Son wept at the death of Lazarus;
look with compassion on <u>*name*</u>'s dearest loved ones,
now bound by sorrow and pain at *her/his* death;
grant the tender healing of your love. Lord, in your mercy,
hear our prayer.

Living God, source of compassion,
our hearts are filled with grief at the death of *name*.
Draw us near to you in faith and to one another in love,
that we may be one with all your saints. Lord, in your mercy,
hear our prayer.

God of salvation, we remember with thanksgiving
all who have died in the hope of the resurrection;
surround them with the light of your presence. Lord, in your mercy,
hear our prayer.

The prayers conclude with these or similar words:
All these things and whatever else you see that we need,
grant us, O God, for the sake of Christ who died and rose again,
and now lives and reigns with you and the Holy Spirit, one God, forever and ever.
Amen.

The Lord's Prayer is prayed.

The leader concludes with a blessing:
Almighty God bless us, defend us from all evil, and bring us to everlasting life.
Amen.

OTHER PRAYERS

These prayers are suitable for use with family and close friends of the deceased at the conclusion of visitation hours, especially in the evening.

A

O Lord, support us all the day long of this troubled life,
until the shadows lengthen and the evening comes and the busy world is hushed,
the fever of life is over, and our work is done.
Then, Lord, in your mercy, grant us a safe lodging, and a holy rest,
and peace at the last; through Jesus Christ our Lord.

B

Lord, it is night. The night is for stillness.
Let us be still in your presence, O God. It is night after a long day.
What has been done, has been done;
what has not been done has not been done; let it be.
The night is dark.
Let our fears of the darkness of the world and of our own lives rest in you.
The night is quiet.
Let the quietness of your peace enfold us, all dear to us, and all who have no peace.
The night heralds the dawn.
Give us hope that we shall see a new day in Christ.

FUNERAL LITURGY

GATHERING

INTRODUCTION

The presiding minister may welcome the assembly with these or similar words:

A p. 78 ▶

Welcome in the name of Jesus the Savior, who died and was raised to new life by the grace of God. We are gathered here to worship, to remember before God our *sister/brother <u>name</u>*, to give thanks for *her/his* life, to commend *her/him* to our merciful redeemer, and to comfort one another in our grief.

GREETING

The ministers meet the coffin and the bereaved at the entrance of the church for the remembrance of baptism. The assembly stands and faces the funeral procession. When the coffin is placed in the church before the liturgy, the remembrance of baptism may be led from the place of the coffin. The presiding minister says to the assembly:

A	B
The grace of our Lord Jesus Christ, the love of God, and the communion of the Holy Spirit be with you all. **And also with you.**	The blessed and holy Trinity, one God, who gives life, salvation, and resurrection, be with you all. **And also with you.**

REMEMBRANCE OF BAPTISM

A pall may be placed on the coffin by family members, pallbearers, or other assisting ministers as the following is said:

A	B
All who are baptized into Christ have put on Christ. In *her/his* baptism *name* was clothed with Christ. In the day of Christ's coming, *she/he* shall be clothed with glory.	When we were baptized in Christ Jesus, we were baptized into his death. We were buried therefore with him by baptism into death, so that as Christ was raised from the dead by the glory of the Father, we too might live a new life. For if we have been united with him in a death like his, we shall certainly be united with him in a resurrection like his.

The presiding minister may sprinkle the coffin with water from the font following each petition:
Let us pray.
Eternal God, maker of heaven and earth, who formed us from the dust of the earth,
who by your breath gave us life: We glorify you.
We glorify you.

Jesus Christ, the resurrection and the life, who suffered death for all humanity,
who rose from the grave to open the way to eternal life: We praise you.
We praise you.

Holy Spirit, author and giver of life, the comforter of all who sorrow,
our sure confidence and everlasting hope: We worship you.
We worship you.

To you, O blessed Trinity, be glory and honor, forever and ever.
Amen.

The procession forms and enters the church, the ministers preceding the coffin. A hymn, psalm, or anthem may be sung during the procession.

PRAYER OF THE DAY

The Lord be with you.
And also with you.

Let us pray.

pp. 78–79 ▶

A

O God of grace and glory,
we remember before you today
our *sister/brother* <u>*name*</u>.
We thank you
for giving *her/him* to us to know and to love
as a companion in our pilgrimage on earth.
In your boundless compassion,
console us who mourn.
Illumine our lives, so we may see in death
the gate to eternal life, that we may continue
our course on earth in confidence
until, by your call, we are reunited
with those who have gone before us;
through your Son, Jesus Christ our Lord.
Amen.

B

Almighty God,
source of all mercy and giver of comfort:
Graciously tend those who mourn,
that, casting all their sorrow on you,
they may know the consolation of your love;
through your Son, Jesus Christ our Lord.
Amen.

Remembrances and expressions of thanksgiving for the life of the deceased may be offered.

WORD

READINGS and RESPONSES

p. 80 ►

Two or three readings are proclaimed. When communion is celebrated, the last is a reading from the gospels. A psalm may be sung or said in response to a reading from the Old Testament. A sung acclamation may precede the reading of the gospel.

SERMON

Silence for reflection follows.

HYMN OF THE DAY

A hymn of the day may be sung.

CREED

The Apostles' Creed may be spoken:
With the whole church, let us confess our faith.
I believe in God the Father almighty,
   creator of heaven and earth.

I believe in Jesus Christ, God's only Son, our Lord,
   who was conceived by the Holy Spirit,
   born of the virgin Mary,
   suffered under Pontius Pilate,
   was crucified, died, and was buried;
   he descended to the dead.
On the third day he rose again;
   he ascended into heaven,
   he is seated at the right hand of the Father,
   and he will come to judge the living and the dead.

I believe in the Holy Spirit,
   the holy catholic church,
   the communion of saints,
   the forgiveness of sins,
   the resurrection of the body,
   and the life everlasting. Amen.

INTERCESSIONS

The intercessory prayers, prepared or adapted for the occasion, may include the following or similar petitions. An assisting minister may lead the prayers:

A *pp. 80–81* ▶

Let us pray to our Lord Jesus Christ who said, "I am the resurrection and the life."

Jesus, fullness of compassion, you consoled Martha and Mary in their distress;
draw near to us who mourn for *name,* and dry the tears of those who weep.
In your mercy,
hear our prayer.

Jesus, man of sorrows, you wept at the grave of Lazarus your friend;
comfort us who mourn.
In your mercy,
hear our prayer.

Jesus, firstborn of the new creation, you raised the dead;
give to our *sister/brother* life eternal.
In your mercy,
hear our prayer.

Jesus, friend of sinners, you promised paradise to the repentant thief;
bring *name* to the joys of heaven.
In your mercy,
hear our prayer.

Jesus, wellspring of life, you washed our *sister/brother* in baptism
and anointed *her/him* with the Holy Spirit;
give *her/him* communion with all your saints.
In your mercy,
hear our prayer.

Jesus, bread of life, you nourished *name* at your table on earth;
welcome *her/him* at your table in the realm of heaven.
In your mercy,
hear our prayer.

Jesus, bright morning star, comfort us in our sorrows at the death of *name*;
let our faith be our consolation, and eternal life our hope. In your mercy,
hear our prayer.

Other petitions may be offered. The presiding minister concludes the prayer:

A

p. 82 ▶

God of all grace, we give you thanks
because by his death our Savior Jesus Christ destroyed the power of death
and by his resurrection opened the kingdom of heaven to all believers.
Make us certain that because he lives we shall live also,
and that neither death nor life, nor things present nor things to come
shall be able to separate us from your love which is in Christ Jesus our Lord,
who lives and reigns with you and the Holy Spirit, one God, now and forever.
Amen.

When the rite does not include holy communion, the liturgy may conclude with the Lord's Prayer, commendation, and sending.

MEAL

When holy communion is celebrated, the liturgy continues with the greeting of peace and the remainder of the liturgy of the meal. Selected texts for the great thanksgiving appear on pp. 82–84.

After the communion, an assisting minister may lead the following or a similar prayer:

PRAYER AFTER COMMUNION

Almighty God, we thank you that in your great love
you have given us a foretaste of your heavenly banquet.
Grant that this sacrament may be to us a comfort in affliction
and a pledge of our inheritance of life eternal
where there is no death, neither sorrow nor crying,
but the fullness of joy with all your saints;
through your Son, Jesus Christ our Lord.
Amen.

COMMENDATION

Remembrances and expressions of thanksgiving for the life of the deceased may be offered if these were not included earlier in the liturgy.

The ministers take their places at the coffin. The presiding minister continues:
Let us commend <u>name</u> to the mercy of God, our maker and redeemer.
Silence is kept.

The presiding minister may place her/his hand on the coffin during the prayer:

A

Into your hands, O merciful Savior,
we commend your servant <u>*name*</u>.
Acknowledge, we humbly beseech you,
a sheep of your own fold,
a lamb of your own flock,
a sinner of your own redeeming.
Receive *her/him*
into the arms of your mercy,
into the blessed rest of everlasting peace,
and into the glorious company
of the saints in light.
Amen.

B   *p. 85* ▶

Into your hands, holy God,
we commend our *sister/brother* <u>*name*</u>.
In this life, through the waters of baptism,
you embraced *her/him*
with your tender love;
now bid *her/him* to enter eternal rest.
Welcome *her/him* into your paradise,
where there will be no more sorrow,
no weeping or pain,
but where *she/he* will enjoy the fullness
of peace and joy in your presence,
forever and ever.
Amen.

A farewell may be sung or said:

A

Now, Lord, you let your servant go in peace:
your word has been fulfilled.
My own eyes have seen the salvation
which you have prepared
in the sight of every people:
a light to reveal you to the nations
and the glory of your people Israel.
Glory to the Father, and to the Son,
and to the Holy Spirit,
as it was in the beginning, is now,
and will be forever. Amen.

B   *p. 85* ▶

Into paradise may the angels lead you.
At your coming may the martyrs receive you,
and bring you into the holy city Jerusalem.
May a choir of angels welcome you,
and where Lazarus is poor no more,
may you have everlasting rest.

SENDING

If the committal occurs at another time, a blessing may precede these words of sending:
Let us go forth in peace.
In the name of Christ. Amen.

The procession forms and leaves the church, the ministers preceding the coffin. As the procession leaves, a hymn, psalm, or anthem may be sung.

COMMITTAL

GATHERING

The ministers precede the coffin to the place of interment. During or at the conclusion of the procession, words of comfort may be spoken and may include any of the following:

Job 19:25	*I know that my Redeemer lives*
Psalm 23	*The Lord is my shepherd*
Psalm 42:1-7	*As a deer longs for flowing streams*
Psalm 121	*I lift up my eyes to the hills*
Romans 14:8	*If we live, we live to the Lord*
Revelation 21:1-4	*Then I saw a new heaven and a new earth*
John 11:25-26a	*I am the resurrection and the life*

Especially at the committal of a child:

Isaiah 40:11	*God will gather the lambs in his arms*
Hosea 11:1, 3-4	*When Israel was a child*
Revelation 7:17	*The Lamb will be their shepherd*
Matthew 19:14	*Let the little children come*

The presiding minister greets those who are gathered:
Grace and peace from our Savior Jesus Christ be with you all.
And also with you.

Let us pray.
A   p. 86 ▶
Holy God, holy and powerful,
by the death and burial of Jesus your anointed,
you have destroyed the power of death
and made holy the resting places of all your people.
Keep our *sister/brother* <u>*name*</u>, whose *body/ashes* we now lay to rest,
in the company of all your saints.
And at the last, O God, raise *her/him* up to share with all the faithful
the endless joy and peace won through the glorious resurrection of Christ our Lord,
who lives and reigns with you and the Holy Spirit, one God, now and forever.
Amen.

WORD

One of the following, or other appropriate texts, may be read:
1 Corinthians 15:51-57   *Where, O death, is your victory*
Philippians 3:20-21   *Our citizenship is in heaven*
John 12:23-26   *Unless a grain of wheat falls into the earth*

Especially at the committal of a child:
Revelation 7:15-17   *God will wipe away every tear*
Revelation 21:3b-4, 7   *I will be their God and they will be my children*

COMMITTAL

Earth may be cast on the coffin as the presiding minister says:
In sure and certain hope of the resurrection to eternal life through our Lord Jesus Christ,
we commend to almighty God our *sister/brother* <u>*name*</u>,
and we commit *her/his* body to *the ground/the deep/the elements/its resting place;*
earth to earth, ashes to ashes, dust to dust.
The Lord bless *her/him* and keep *her/him.*
The Lord's face shine on *her/him* with grace and mercy.
The Lord look upon *her/him* with favor and give *her/him* ✝ peace.
Amen.

Or, when ashes are interred, the presiding minister says:
In sure and certain hope of the resurrection to eternal life through our Lord Jesus Christ,
we commend to almighty God our *sister/brother* <u>*name*</u>,
and we commit *her/his* ashes to their final resting place.
The Lord bless *her/him* and keep *her/him.*
The Lord's face shine on *her/him* with grace and mercy.
The Lord look upon *her/him* with favor and give *her/him* ✝ peace.

The following or another response may be sung, or the minister may say:
A
Rest eternal grant *her/him,* O Lord;
and let light perpetual shine upon *her/him.*

p. 85 ▸

SENDING

An assisting minister leads the assembly in prayer:
In the peace of Christ, let us pray,
saying, Be gracious to us.

Jesus, Savior of the world,
be gracious to us.
By your incarnation and nativity,
be gracious to us.
By your prayers and tears,
be gracious to us.
By your grief and anguish,
be gracious to us.
By your cross and suffering,
be gracious to us.
By your atoning death,
be gracious to us.
By your rest in the grave,
be gracious to us.
By your triumphant resurrection,
be gracious to us.
By your presence with your people,
be gracious to us.
By the promise of your coming at the end of the ages,
be gracious to us.

The presiding minister concludes the prayers:
A   p. 86 ▶
O Lord, support us all the day long of this troubled life,
until the shadows lengthen, and the evening comes, and the busy world is hushed,
and the fever of life is over, and our work is done.
Then, O Lord, in your mercy, grant us a safe lodging,
and a holy rest, and peace at the last; through Jesus Christ our Lord.
Amen.

The Lord's Prayer may be prayed.

BLESSING AND DISMISSAL

The assembly is blessed and sent forth.

A

Almighty God, Father, ✛ Son, and Holy
Spirit, bless you now and forever.
Amen.

Go in peace. Serve the Lord.
Thanks be to God.

B

The God of peace, who brought back
from the dead our Lord Jesus,
the great shepherd of the sheep,
make you complete in everything good
so that you may do God's will,
working among you
that which is well-pleasing in God's sight;
through Jesus Christ,
to whom be glory forever and ever.
Amen.

Scripture Readings

AT THE PROCESSIONS

Psalm 23	*The Lord is my shepherd*
Psalm 90	*You have been our dwelling place in all generations*
Psalm 118	*God's steadfast love endures forever*
Psalm 130	*Out of the depths I cry to you*
Isaiah 41:10	*Do not be afraid, for I am with you*
Romans 14:7-9	*Whether we live or die, we are the Lord's*
Revelation 1:17-18	*Do not be afraid, I am the first and the last*
Revelation 14:13	*Blessed are the dead who die in the Lord*
Matthew 11:28-29	*Come to me, all you who are weary*
John 11:25-26	*I am the resurrection and the life*
John 14:27	*Peace I leave with you*

OLD TESTAMENT

Job 19:23-27a	*I know that my Redeemer lives*
Ecclesiastes 3:1-15	*For everything there is a season*
Isaiah 25:6-9	*God will swallow up death forever*
Isaiah 40:1-11, 28-31	*Comfort, O comfort my people*
Isaiah 43:1-3a, 18-19, 25	*I am about to do a new thing*
Isaiah 55:1-3, 6-13	*Everyone who thirsts, come to the waters*
Isaiah 61:1-3	*The spirit of the Lord God is upon me*
Jeremiah 31:8-13	*I will turn their mourning into joy*
Lamentations 3:22-26, 31-33	*The steadfast love of the Lord never ceases*

PSALM

Psalm 42:1-7	*As a deer longs for flowing streams*
Psalm 46:1-7	*God is our refuge and strength*
Psalm 121	*I lift up my eyes to the hills*
Psalm 143	*Hear my prayer, O Lord; give ear to my supplications*

NEW TESTAMENT

Romans 5:1-11	*Peace with God through our Lord Jesus Christ*
Romans 8:31-35, 37-39	*Who will separate us from the love of Christ*
1 Corinthians 15:12-26	*Christ, the firstfruits, has been raised from the dead*
2 Corinthians 4:7-18	*We have this treasure in clay jars*
1 Thessalonians 4:13-14, 18	*We do not want you to be uninformed about those who have died*
Hebrews 12:1-2	*We are surrounded by so great a cloud of witnesses*
1 Peter 1:3-9	*A living hope through the resurrection of Jesus Christ from the dead*
Revelation 7:9-17	*God will wipe away every tear*
Revelation 21:2-7	*I saw the holy city, the new Jerusalem*
Revelation 22:1-5	*The Lord God will be their light*

GOSPEL

Matthew 5:1-10	*Blessed are those who mourn*
Matthew 11:25-30	*Come to me, all you who are weary*
Mark 16:1-7	*The resurrection of Christ*
Luke 24:1-9, 36-43	*The resurrection of Christ*
John 1:1-5, 9-14	*The light shines in the darkness*
John 6:37-40	*I will raise them up on the last day*
John 10:11-16	*I am the good shepherd*
John 11:21-27	*I am the resurrection and the life*
John 14:1-6	*In my Father's house are many rooms*
John 14:25-27	*Peace I leave with you; my peace I give to you*

Especially at the death of a child:

OLD TESTAMENT

Isaiah 40:1, 6-11	*God will gather the lambs*
Isaiah 43:1-3a, 5-7	*I have called you by name, you are mine*
Isaiah 65:17-20, 23-25	*I am about to create a new heaven and a new earth*
Isaiah 66:10-14	*As a mother comforts her child*

PSALM

Psalm 23	*The Lord is my shepherd*
Psalm 42:1-7	*As a deer longs for flowing streams*
Psalm 121	*I lift up my eyes to the hills*
Psalm 139:7-12	*The gracious omnipresence of the Lord*
Psalm 142:1-6	*With my voice I cry to the Lord*

NEW TESTAMENT

Romans 8:31-35, 37-39	*Who will separate us from the love of Christ*
1 Thessalonians 4:13-14, 18	*We do not want you to be uninformed about those who have died*
1 John 3:1-2	*See what love the Father has given us*

GOSPEL

Matthew 5:1-10	*Blessed are those who mourn*
Matthew 18:1-5, 10-14	*A child is the greatest in the kingdom*
Mark 10:13-16	*Let the little children come to me*
John 10:11-16	*I am the good shepherd*

Supplemental Materials

INTRODUCTION

B

Blessed be the God and Father of our Lord Jesus Christ,
the source of all mercy and the God of all consolation.
God comforts us in our sorrows so that we can comfort others
with the consolation we ourselves have received from God.

PRAYER OF THE DAY

C

Eternal God, we bless you for the great company of those
who have finished their course in faith and now rest from their labor.
We praise you for those dear to us whom we name before you. . . .
Especially we thank you for *name,*
whom you have graciously received into your presence.
By your presence lead us through our years,
and bring us at last with all your saints
into the joy of your eternal home;
through Jesus Christ our Lord.
Amen.

D

O God, your days are without end
and your mercies cannot be counted.
Make us aware of the shortness and uncertainty of human life,
and let your Holy Spirit lead us
in holiness and righteousness all the days of our life,
so that, when we have served you in our generation,
we may be gathered to our ancestors,
having the testimony of a good conscience,
in communion with your church,
in the confidence of a certain faith,
in the comfort of a holy hope,
in favor with you, our God,
and in peace with all humanity;
through Jesus Christ our Lord.
Amen.

E (at the death of a child)

Gracious God, we come before you this day in pain and sorrow.
We grieve the loss of *name*, a precious human life.
Give your grace to those who grieve (especially *name/s*),
that they may find comfort in your presence
and be strengthened by your Spirit.
Be with this family as they mourn,
and draw them together in your healing love;
in the name of one who suffered, died, and rose for us,
Jesus our Savior.
Amen.

F (at a sudden death)

O God of hope and healing,
in baptism you have woven us all into the communion of saints.
Today we come to you in grief and shock at the sudden death of *name*.
Help us accept the reality of what has happened,
and enable us to find comfort and peace in your presence
and in the love of family and friends.
Lead us out of darkness into the joyous Light of glory,
Jesus Christ our Lord.
Amen.

G (at a death by suicide)

Compassionate and understanding God,
we entrust to you *name*, who has died by *her/his* own hand.
Comfort us in the assurance
that *she/he* is now fully enfolded by your baptismal grace and care.
Be with all who love *her/him*;
console all who are sorrowing.
Give them light in their darkness,
comfort in their grief,
and hope in the resurrection to eternal life
through Jesus Christ our Lord.
Amen.

H (at a death by suicide)

Lord Jesus Christ, you knew the agony of dying alone and abandoned.
We cannot know the agony which led *name* to take *her/his* own life.
We grieve that we were unable to sustain *her/him* in *her/his* desolation.
Console us in the face of death's apparent triumph,
forgive us our failures,
and give us the assurance that, in our pain, you can bring hope;
for your mercy's sake.
Amen.

GOSPEL ACCLAMATION

A

Alleluia. Jesus Christ is the firstborn from the dead;
to him be glory and power forever and ever. Alleluia.

B

[Alleluia.] O God, you have been our refuge
from one generation to another. [Alleluia.]

INTERCESSIONS

B
Let us pray.

Almighty God,
in holy baptism you have woven your chosen people together
in one communion of saints in the mystical body of your Son.
Give to your whole church in heaven and on earth your light and peace.
God of mercy,
hear our prayer.

May all who have been baptized into Christ's death and resurrection
die to sin and rise to share the new life in Christ.
God of mercy,
hear our prayer.

Mercifully grant to all who mourn
a sure and certain hope in your loving care,
that, casting all their grief on you,
they may have strength for the days and weeks ahead.
God of mercy,
hear our prayer.

Help us in our present confusion and loss,
and enable us to trust in the communion of saints,
the forgiveness of our sins, and the life everlasting.
God of mercy,
hear our prayer.

C
In the peace of God, let us pray.

God of mercy, Lord of life,
you have made us in your image to reflect your truth and light:
We give you thanks for *name,* for the grace and mercy *she/he* received from you,
for all that was good in *her/his* life, for the memories we treasure today.
(Especially we thank you . . .)
silence
Lord, in your mercy,
hear our prayer.

You promised eternal life to those who believe.
Remember your servant *name*
and bring all who rest in Christ into the fullness of your reign,
where sins have been forgiven and death is no more.
silence
Lord, in your mercy,
hear our prayer.

Your mighty power brings joy out of grief and life out of death.
Look in mercy on all who mourn.
Give us patient faith in times of sorrow.
Strengthen us with the knowledge of your love.
silence
Lord, in your mercy,
hear our prayer.

You are tender toward your children
and your mercy is over all your works.
Heal the memories of hurt and failure.
Give us grace to use wisely our time here on earth,
to turn to Christ and follow in his steps
in the way that leads to everlasting life.
silence
Lord, in your mercy,
hear our prayer.

CONCLUSION TO INTERCESSIONS

B (at the death of a child)

Creator of all, by your mighty power you gave us life,
and in baptism you have given us new life in Christ Jesus.
We commend *name* to your merciful arms, trusting in your mercy.
Help us to remember the joy that *she/he* brought to us,
and guide us through our present darkness with the unfailing light of your Christ.
Amen.

C (at a sudden death, at a suicide)

God of compassion, comfort us with the great power of your love
as we mourn the sudden death of *name*. In our grief and confusion,
help us to find peace in the knowledge of your mercy and grace to all your children,
and give us light to guide us into the assurance of your love;
through Jesus Christ our Lord.
Amen.

PROPER PREFACE

It is indeed right and salutary
that we should at all times and in all places offer thanks and praise,
O Lord, almighty and ever-living God.
In Christ who rose from the dead our hope of resurrection dawned.
The sting of death has been removed by the glorious promise of his risen life.
And so with the church on earth and the hosts of heaven,
we praise your name and join their unending hymn:
The Sanctus follows.

EUCHARISTIC PRAYER

A

Holy God, holy and mighty, holy and immortal:
Surrounded by evil and bordered by death
we appeal to you, our sovereign, our wisdom, and our judge.

We praise you for Christ, victor over death,
who proclaimed your reign of peace
and promised an end to injustice and harm.

In the night in which he was betrayed
our Lord Jesus took bread, and gave thanks;
broke it and gave it to his disciples, saying:
Take and eat; this is my body given for you.
Do this for the remembrance of me.

Again, after supper, he took the cup, gave thanks,
and gave it for all to drink, saying:
This cup is the new covenant in my blood,
shed for you and for all people for the forgiveness of sin.
Do this for the remembrance of me.

Remembering, therefore,
the sacrifice of his life and death
and the victory of his resurrection,
we await with *name* and all the saints
his loving redemption of our suffering world.

Let us proclaim the mystery of faith:
Christ has died. Christ is risen. Christ will come again.

Send your Spirit on these gifts of bread and wine
and on all who share in the body and blood of your Son.
Teach us your mercy and justice,
and make all things new in Christ;
through whom all glory and honor is yours,
almighty Father, with the Holy Spirit,
in your holy church, both now and forever.
Amen.

B

You are holy, O God of majesty,
and holy is your Son, Jesus Christ our Lord.
He lived as one of us, and knew our joy, our pain and sorrow, and our death.
By his death on the cross you revealed that your love has no limit.
By raising him from death you conquered the last enemy,
crushed all evil powers, and gave new life to the world.

In the night in which he was betrayed
our Lord Jesus took bread, and gave thanks;
broke it and gave it to his disciples, saying:
Take and eat; this is my body given for you.
Do this for the remembrance of me.

Again, after supper, he took the cup, gave thanks,
and gave it for all to drink, saying:
This cup is the new covenant in my blood,
shed for you and for all people for the forgiveness of sin.
Do this for the remembrance of me.

Remembering your gracious acts in Jesus Christ,
we take from your creation this bread and wine
and joyfully celebrate his death and resurrection,
as we await the day of his coming.

Let us proclaim the mystery of faith:
Christ has died. Christ is risen. Christ will come again.

Gracious God,
pour out your Holy Spirit upon us,
and upon these gifts of bread and wine,
that the bread we break and the cup we bless
may be the communion of the body and blood of Christ.
By your Spirit unite us with the living Christ
and with all who are baptized in his name.

Remember our *sister/brother <u>name</u>,*
whose baptism is now complete in death.
Bring *her/him* into your eternal joy and light,
together with all who have died in the peace of Christ;
through whom, and with whom, and in whom,
in the unity of the Holy Spirit,
all glory and honor is yours, almighty God, now and forever.
Amen.

COMMENDATION

C

God our creator and redeemer,
by your power Christ conquered death and entered into glory.
Confident in his victory and claiming his promises,
we entrust *name* to your mercy in the name of Jesus our Lord,
who died and is alive and reigns with you, now and forever.

D

Name, our companion in faith,
we entrust you to God.
Go forth from this world
in the love of God who created you,
in the mercy of Jesus who died for you,
in the power of the Holy Spirit
who receives and protects you.
May you rest in peace and rise in glory,
where pain and grief are banished,
and life and joy are yours forever.

SONGS OF FAREWELL
Commendation, Committal

C

Rest eternal grant unto *her/him*, O Lord;
and let light perpetual shine on *her/him*.

D

Give rest, O Christ, to your servant with your saints,
where sorrow and pain are no more,
neither sighing, but life everlasting.

E

The Lord shall watch over your going out and your coming in,
from this time forth forevermore.

F

All of us go down to the dust,
yet even at the grave we make our song:
Alleluia, alleluia, alleluia.

COMMITTAL
Prayer at the Gathering

B

O loving God, you are gracious and tender-hearted.
You have created all people, and you love all whom you have made.
Have mercy on *name,* and take *her/him* into your arms of grace.
Grant to *her/his* family and friends light in this time of darkness,
and comfort in this time of sadness; through Jesus Christ, our Lord.
Amen.

COMMITTAL
Concluding Prayer

B

Merciful God, you heal the broken in heart
and bind up the wounds of the afflicted.
Strengthen us in our weakness,
calm our troubled spirits,
and dispel our doubts and fears.
In Christ's rising from the dead,
you conquered death and opened the gates to everlasting life.
Renew our trust in you that by the power of your love
we shall one day be brought together again with our *sister/brother name.*
Grant this, we pray through Jesus Christ our Lord.
Amen.

C

Father, the death of *name* has plunged our lives into darkness.
Separated from *her/him,* we are broken; we are adrift.
Grant us your healing grace for the days ahead.
Give us confidence that *name* is safe, that *her/his* life is complete with you.
Deepen our trust that in Christ you have bridged the great chasm that has opened between us,
and that at the last you will bring us together again with all the faithful
into the light of your presence. We ask this through Jesus Christ our Lord.
Amen.

D

Merciful God, source of our healing,
as your servant Mary stood at the foot of the cross,
we stand before you with broken hearts and tear-filled eyes.
Keep us mindful that you know our pain,
and lead us to see your resurrection power already at work in *name.*
In your time, raise us from our grief
even as you have promised to raise *name* to life eternal;
through Jesus Christ our Savior.
Amen.

OTHER PRAYERS

A (one who dies by violence)

God our deliverer, gather our horror and pity for the death of your child *name* into the compass of your wisdom and strength, that through the night we may seek and do what is right, and when morning comes trust ourselves to your cleansing justice and new life; through Christ our Savior.

B (one who dies by violence)

God, do not hide your face from us in our anger and grief for the death of *name*. Renew us in hope that your justice will roll down like mighty waters and joy spring up from the broken ground in a living stream, through Jesus our Savior.

C (a child who dies by violence)

Loving God, Jesus gathered your little ones in his arms and blessed them. Have pity on those who mourn for *name*, an innocent slaughtered by the violence of our fallen world. Be with us as we struggle with the mysteries of life and death; in our pain, bring your comfort, and in our sorrow, bring your hope and your promise of new life, in the name of Jesus our Savior.

D (one who dies by suicide)

All knowing and eternal God, come to our help as we mourn for *name*. We know only in part, we love imperfectly, and we fail to ease one another's pain as you intend. But you are always merciful, and so we put our trust in you and ask the courage to go on; through our Savior Jesus Christ, who suffered for us, and whom you raised to new life.

E (one who dies by suicide)

Out of the depths we cry to you, merciful God, for your child *name*. Meet our confusion with your peace, our anger with forgiveness, and our sorrow with consolation. Help us acknowledge the mystery that our lives are hid with Christ in you, whose compassion is over all you have made.

F (those who mourn)

Most loving God: The death of your Son has opened to us a new and living way. Give us hope to overcome our despair; help us to surrender *name* to your keeping, and let our sorrow find comfort in your care; through the name and presence of Jesus our Savior.

ADDITIONAL PRAYERS IN DEVELOPMENT

Death as release from suffering
Death of an elderly person
When ashes are scattered
End of the first year of bereavement

Resources for the Commendation of a Stillborn Child

When an infant is stillborn or dies shortly after birth, the following resources may be useful in addition to or in place of various elements of the funeral liturgy. Some of these resources may also be useful in the case of a miscarriage.

INTRODUCTION

Welcome in the name of Jesus the Savior, who died and was raised to new life by the grace of God. We come to seek the comfort of God as we mourn the death of a child, known to the mother who carried *her/him,* known to all those who have anticipated *her/his* birth in hope and expectation. We commend *her/him* to our merciful redeemer, even as we console one another in our grief.

NAMING

Parents may choose to name their child publicly.

The presiding minister says:
The word of the Lord came to Jeremiah saying, "Before I formed you in the womb, I knew you." The name Jesus was given to the child of Mary, the Son of God, as a sign of salvation for all people. The naming of this child reminds us of God's care for *her/him* and helps us remember *her/his* coming among us.

The presiding minister addresses parents:
What do you name your child?
Parents respond: We name *her/him* <u>name</u>.

Parents or others may also comment on the significance of the name.

PRAYER OF THE DAY

Out of the depths we cry to you, O loving God.
Enable us to find in Christ the faith to trust your care,
so that even in the pain of losing this little life,
we may not walk alone through the valley of the shadow of death,
through Christ our Lord.
Amen.

READINGS

In addition to the readings listed on pages 76–77, the following may be suitable:

Deuteronomy 33:27a	*The eternal God is your dwelling place*
Isaiah 40:27-31	*Those who wait on the Lord will renew their strength*
Psalm 139:1-15	*Your right hand will hold me fast*
Romans 8:26-27	*The Spirit intercedes for us with sighs too deep for words*
1 John 3:12	*We are children of God*
Luke 18:15-17	*Jesus blesses the children*

COMMENDATION

Merciful God, your Spirit intercedes for us even when we do not know how to pray.
Be present among us now that we might commend *name* / *this child* / *this pregnancy*
into your loving care and, by your presence, find comfort;
through Jesus Christ, your Son, our Savior.
Amen.

[Name,] Child of God, we entrust you to God who created you,
who formed us all out of the dust of the earth.
Amen.

May this child *[name]* and all the departed, through the mercy of God, rest in peace.
Amen.

OTHER PRAYERS

A (at the death of an infant)
God our creator, you called into being this fragile life, which had seemed to us so full of
promise. Give to *name,* whom we commit to your care, abundant life in your presence,
and to us, who grieve for hopes destroyed, courage to bear our loss; through Jesus Christ
our Savior.

B (at the event of a miscarriage)
O God, who gathered Rachel's tears over her lost children, hear now the sorrow and distress of *name/s* for the death of *their* expected child. In the darkness of loss, stretch out to
them the strength of your arm and renewed assurance of your love; through your own suffering and risen Child Jesus.

C (for a stillbirth, or a child who dies soon after birth)
Heavenly Father, your love for all children is strong and enduring. We were not able to
know *name* as we hoped. Yet you knew *her/him* growing in *her/his* mother's womb, and
she/he is not lost to you. In the midst of our sadness, we thank you that *name* is with you
now.

D (for a mother and loved ones of a child who has died near birth)

Loving God, we thank you that in your mercy you brought your daughter *name* through childbirth in safety. We pray that *name/s* will know your support in this time of trouble and enjoy your protection always; through Jesus Christ our Savior.

E (for those who mourn)

Merciful God, you grant to children an abundant entrance into your kingdom. In your compassion, comfort those who mourn for *name*, and grant us grace to conform our lives to *her/his* innocence and faith, that at length, united with *her/him,* we may stand in your presence in the fullness of joy; for the sake of Jesus Christ.

Notes on the Rites

From care for the dying person to care for the mourners at significant anniversaries of death, the church's ministry at the time of death is a continuum that includes a number of occasions for pastoral care and worship by smaller groups as well as the larger Christian assembly. The rites in this provisional volume, focused on the public occasions that immediately follow death, are intended primarily for use with the body or cremated remains of a baptized Christian present and with the funeral liturgy taking place in a church. Some possible adaptations for use as a memorial service or with an unbaptized person are suggested in the rite or in these notes. Other adaptations for particular circumstances are a natural part of pastoral ministry at the time of death, and are beyond the scope of this provisional resource.

Comforting the Bereaved

GENERAL
Although the setting for this rite is often a funeral home or the home of the deceased, particularly in connection with a scheduled time when family members receive visitors (a "wake," in some traditions), some churches are exploring the possibilities for providing room in the church building (usually in an area other than the worship space) for such visitation to take place. The rite may be led at a scheduled time during the visitation when those present can participate. A pastor or another person may lead the service. Especially when the group is small, remaining seated throughout the rite may be conducive to prayer, silence, reflection, and conversation with one another. Usually no printed materials will be needed for participants.

GATHERING
An invitation for those present to gather for prayer and remembrance may be concluded with a time of silence and the words of the Kyrie in either its western (Lord, have mercy) or eastern (Holy God) form, followed by an opening prayer.

WORD
One or more brief readings from the scriptures by the leader or others present may be followed by a time of mutual consolation and conversation. The leader may introduce this time by recalling and giving thanks for some aspect of the life of the deceased, perhaps relating it to a scripture reading, and then inviting others to share memories and thanksgivings as well as expressions of grief and loss, in a spontaneous fashion.

PRAYER
The leader may offer some or all of the prayers printed in the rite, and other thanksgivings and intercessions may be invited from those present. The prayers conclude with the Lord's Prayer in a version likely to be known by heart among those present (unless printed materials are provided).

Funeral Liturgy

GATHERING

Words of introduction such as those included in the rite offer the opportunity for a gracious welcome by the presiding minister prior to meeting the procession at the entrance to the church.

References to the coffin in this liturgy include also the possibility of a smaller container for the ashes of the deceased when cremation has taken place. Whether this container is an urn or the urn is placed in an ossuary (typically a wooden box that may have handles for carrying), it may be placed on a table and covered with a pall that is smaller than the one used for a larger coffin. At the various processions in these rites the urn or ossuary may be carried by one of the ministers or, when equipped with suitable handles, by several pallbearers.

The elements used in the gathering rite and their order depend a great deal on the space where the liturgy takes place and the particular circumstances. For example, the placement of the baptismal font may influence where the placing of the pall and the remembrance of baptism best take place. The bereaved (often the immediate family) may take part in the procession or may be seated in the assembly prior to the service.

When the liturgy is a memorial service, some or all of the liturgical texts provided may be used without the accompanying actions. When the deceased was not baptized, the remembrance of baptism is omitted and prayer of the day B may be used. A variety of optional prayers of the day is provided for various circumstances.

When a child is stillborn or dies shortly after birth, the naming rite on page 88 may replace the remembrance of baptism.

The gathering may conclude with a time when relatives or associates of the deceased comment briefly in thanksgiving for and remembrance of the one who has died.

WORD

Readings may be drawn from the list of suggested readings on pages 76–77. Proclaiming a reading is another significant way to engage the participation of family members or friends. The sermon by the presiding minister will normally be a part of the service.

The hymn of the day is the principal opportunity for the assembly to express grief and proclaim hope in song. The creed may be omitted in particular circumstances, such as when the deceased was unbaptized or the assembly is not predominantly Christian.

MEAL

When communion is a part of the liturgy, the sacrament is celebrated with the whole assembly, beginning with the greeting of peace. One of the proper prayers of thanksgiving (see pages 83–84) may be used.

COMMENDATION

The commendation is led from the place of the coffin (or, at a memorial service, from the place where the prayers were led). A substantial time of silence is kept prior to the words of commendation. Commendation C is for use when the deceased was not baptized.

SENDING

The assembly stands for the sending. A procession may follow to the place of interment.

Committal

GENERAL

Committal may take place immediately following the funeral liturgy or at a later time. It may also precede the funeral liturgy; for example, when the deceased is interred in one location and the memorial service takes place at a later time in another location, or when the deceased is interred immediately following death. Usually no printed materials will be needed for participants in this rite; the leader may prompt the responses of those gathered.

The prayers and readings in this rite are also resources for family members and friends to use when ashes are scattered at a place where it is not possible for a larger assembly to be present.

GATHERING

Especially when those gathered are walking some distance to the place of burial, scripture passages such as those noted on page 70 may be spoken by a leader along the way. A greeting and prayer gather those who are present. Prayer at the gathering B may be used when the deceased was an unbaptized person.

WORD

When the committal immediately follows the funeral liturgy, one or more brief readings may suffice. When the committal takes place at another time, the liturgy of the word may be more extended, and may include a brief homily and remembrance of the deceased.

COMMITTAL

The words and actions accompanying the committal may be adapted to the circumstances. Especially when the coffin can be placed into the ground before the words of committal, the casting of earth is a fitting gesture. Other adaptations may be appropriate when a coffin is placed in a mausoleum, when ashes are interred in a columbarium, when ashes are placed in a memorial garden, or when ashes are scattered at land or sea.

SENDING

The litany may be led by an assisting minister. The prayers may conclude with the Lord's Prayer in a version likely to be known by heart among those present (unless printed materials are provided).

Acknowledgments

Life Passages: Marriage, Healing, Funeral editorial team: Marcia Cox, Donald J. Luther, Mark Strobel; Michael Burk, Cheryl Dieter, Martin A. Seltz, Frank Stoldt (Renewing Worship project management staff).

Life Passages: Marriage, Healing, Funeral development panel: Robert Albers, Herbert Anderson, Laura Bernardo, Susan Briehl, Lorraine Brugh, Joseph Donnella II, Jan Erickson-Pearson, Frederick Graham, Thomas Graham, Emmanuel Grantson, Robert Hawkins, Karen Johnson-Lefsrud, Victor Jortack, Galen Knutson, Andre Lavergne, Gordon Lathrop, Mark Luttio, Rafael Malpica-Padilla, Andrew Paulsen, Janet Peterman, Mindy Quivik, Elaine Ramshaw, Adele Resmer, Robert A. Rimbo, Gwen Sayler, Thomas H. Schattauer, Stephen Schmidt, Sheldon Sorge, S. Anita Stauffer, Karen Walhof, Donald Wisner.

Design and production: Jessica Hillstrom, production; Carolyn Porter of The Kantor Group, Inc., book design; Nicholas Markell, logo design.

Book of Common Worship, © 1993 Westminster John Knox Press: prayer after communion (marriage), 10; introduction (marriage) B, abridged, 12; anointing B, 30; litany for healing B, 34–35; blessing of oil B, 36; anointing C, 37; prayer at remembrance of baptism, 67; intercessions (funeral) A, 69; conclusion to intercessions (funeral) C, 82; eucharistic prayer (funeral) B, 84; concluding prayer (committal) B, 86; prayer of the day (commendation of a stillborn child), 88

A Christian Celebration of Marriage, © 1995 Consultation on Common Texts: introduction A, 5; declaration of intention A, 5–6; vows A, 7; blessing of rings A, 7; nuptial blessing A, 8; prayer of the day B, 14; nuptial blessing B, 16; intercessions B, 17–18

Common Worship: Services and Prayers for the Church of England, © 2000 The Archbishops' Council: blessing of rings B, 15; proper preface (funeral), 82; commendation (funeral) B, 84

Enriching Our Worship 2: Ministry with the Sick or Dying, Burial of a Child, © 2000 The Church Pension Fund: blessing of oil A, 29; introduction to laying on of hands, 30; laying on of hands B, 30; conclusion of litany for healing B, 35; blessing (healing) B, 38; litany at the time of death, 41; gathering prayer (commendation of the dying) B–C, 44; commendation of the dying C, 44; gathering prayers and litany when life-sustaining care ends, 45, 46–47; other prayers when life-sustaining care ends A–C, 49; prayer of the day (funeral) E, 79; commendation (funeral) C, 85; concluding prayer (committal) D, 86; other prayers (funeral) A–F, 87; other prayers (commendation of a stillborn child) A–E, 89–90

Holy Baptism and Related Rites, Renewing Worship, vol. 3, © 2002 Augsburg Fortress: greeting (funeral) B, 66; remembrance of baptism A, 66

Lutheran Book of Worship and *Lutheran Book of Worship* Ministers Edition, © 1978 Lutheran Church in America, The American Lutheran Church, The Evangelical Lutheran Church of Canada, and The Lutheran Church—Missouri Synod: prayer of the day (marriage) A, 6; exchange of rings A, 7; marriage acclamation, 7; marriage introduction C, adapt., 12; vows B, 14; vows D, 15; nuptial blessing E, 17; intercessions B, 17–18; prayer at the commendation of the dying, 42; other prayers when life-sustaining care ends D, 49; words of forgiveness A, 51; remembrance of baptism B, 66; prayer of the day (funeral) A–B, 67; conclusion to intercessions (funeral) A, 70; commendation (funeral) A, 71; committal, 72; introduction (funeral) B, 78; prayer of the day (funeral) D, 78; gospel acclamation (funeral) A, 80; song of farewell C, 85

Moravian Book of Worship, © 1995 Interprovincial Board of Publication and Communications: sending litany (committal), 74

A New Zealand Prayer Book / He Karakia Mihinare o Aotearoa, © 1989 The Anglican Church in Aotearoa, New Zealand, and Polynesia: prayer of the day (marriage) C, 14; other prayers (comforting the bereaved) B, 65

Occasional Services, © 1982 Association of Evangelical Lutheran Churches, Lutheran Church in America, The American Lutheran Church, The Evangelical Lutheran Church of Canada: laying on of hands A, 30; prayer after anointing A, 30; prayer after communion (healing) B, 38; other prayers (healing) A–H, K–L, 38–39; gathering prayer (commendation of the dying) A, 40; prayers and words of commendation for the dying, 42; commendation of the dying D, 44; gathering prayers (comforting the bereaved) A–D, 63; prayer at the gathering (committal) A, 72; blessing (committal), 75

Pastoral Care of the Sick: Rites of Anointing and Viaticum, © 1982 International Committee on English in the Liturgy (ICEL): prayer after anointing B, 30; blessing A, 31

Praying Together, © 1988 English Language Liturgical Consultation (ELLC): Apostles' Creed, 68; "Now, Lord, you let your servant go in peace," 71

Proposed Order for Christian Marriage, Reformed Church in America: declaration of intention B (couple), 13; declaration of intention C (question to parents), 13

"Remembrance and Commendation: A Rite to Speak to Losses in Pregnancy," prepared by Janet Peterman, in *Lutheran Partners* 4:4 (July–August 1988): naming and commendation (commendation of a stillborn child), 88, 89

Service Book and Hymnal, © 1958, administered by Augsburg Fortress: marriage blessing A, 10

Sundays and Seasons 2001, © 2000 Augsburg Fortress: anointing A, 30

This Far by Faith: An African American Resource for Worship, © 1999 Augsburg Fortress: notes on the rite (marriage), 21, paragraph 5

The United Methodist Book of Worship, © 1992 The United Methodist Publishing House: prayer of the day (funeral) C, 78

With One Voice Leaders Edition, © 1995 Augsburg Fortress: eucharistic prayer (funeral) A, 83

For Further Reading

GENERAL REFERENCE

Anderson, Herbert, and Edward Foley. *Mighty Stories, Dangerous Rituals: Weaving Together the Human and the Divine.* San Francisco: Jossey-Bass, 1998.

Bradshaw, Paul F., and Lawrence A. Hoffman. *Life Cycles in Jewish and Christian Worship.* Notre Dame: University of Notre Dame Press, 1996.

Hawkins, Robert D. "Occasional Services: Border Crossings." *Inside Out: Worship in an Age of Mission.* Ed. Thomas H. Schattauer. Minneapolis: Fortress Press, 1999.

Ramshaw, Elaine. *Ritual and Pastoral Care.* Philadelphia: Fortress Press, 1987.

Senn, Frank C. *Christian Liturgy.* Minneapolis: Fortress Press, 1997. Chapter 18.

Stauffer, S. Anita, ed. *Baptism, Rites of Passage, and Culture.* Geneva: Lutheran World Federation, 1999.

The Use of the Means of Grace: A Statement on the Practice of Word and Sacrament. Evangelical Lutheran Church in America. Minneapolis: Augsburg Fortress, 1997.

Van Gennep, Arnold. *The Rites of Passage.* Tr. Monika B. Vizedom and Gabrielle L. Caffee. Chicago: University of Chicago Press, 1960.

MARRIAGE

Baker, J. Robert, Joni Reiff Gibley, and Kevin Charles Gibley, eds. *A Marriage Sourcebook.* Chicago: Liturgy Training Publications, 1994.

Consultation on Common Texts. *A Christian Celebration of Marriage: An Ecumenical Liturgy.* Rev. ed. Minneapolis: Augsburg Fortress, 1995.

Cooke, Bernard, ed. *Christian Marriage. Alternative Futures for Worship,* vol. 5. Collegeville: Liturgical Press, 1987.

Stevenson, Kenneth. *Nuptial Blessing: A Study of Christian Marriage Rites.* New York: Oxford University Press, 1983.

HEALING

Dudley, Martin, and Geoffrey Rowell, eds. *The Oil of Gladness: Anointing in the Christian Tradition.* London: SPCK and Collegeville: Liturgical Press, 1993.

Fink, Peter E., S.J., ed. *Anointing of the Sick. Alternative Futures for Worship,* vol. 7. Collegeville: Liturgical Press, 1987.

Kelsey, Morton. *Healing and Christianity.* Minneapolis: Augsburg Fortress, 1995.

FUNERAL

Enriching Our Worship 2: Ministry with the Sick or Dying, Burial of a Child. Supplemental Liturgical Materials prepared by The Standing Commission on Liturgy and Music. New York: Church Publishing Incorporated, 2000.

Sloyan, Virginia, ed. *A Sourcebook about Christian Death.* Chicago: Liturgy Training Publications, 1990.

RENEWING WORSHIP

A series of provisional resources produced by the Evangelical Lutheran Church in America as part of the Renewing Worship multiyear project to prepare new primary worship resources. Each includes the opportunity for feedback and response.

Congregational Song: Proposals for Renewal. Renewing Worship, vol. 1. Minneapolis: Augsburg Fortress, 2001.
> Over eighty hymns, many of them reproducible for use in congregational bulletins, present various strategies for the renewal and revision of the treasured tradition of the church's song.

Principles for Worship. Renewing Worship, vol. 2. Minneapolis: Augsburg Fortress, 2002.
> Guiding principles for language, music, preaching, and worship space, developed through a churchwide consultative process. The principles, with their supporting background and applications, are based upon the content and the model of *The Use of the Means of Grace*, which is included in full as an appendix.

Holy Baptism and Related Rites. Renewing Worship, vol. 3. Minneapolis: Augsburg Fortress, 2002.
> Worship patterns, rites, and supplemental materials for baptism, affirmation of baptism, and corporate orders of confession and forgiveness.

Forthcoming volumes in the series (projected dates and content subject to change):

New Hymns and Songs. Renewing Worship, vol. 5 (2003).
> Approximately 150 hymns, songs, and canticles for provisional use, this resource will contain primarily materials that did not appear in *Lutheran Book of Worship* and *With One Voice*.

Holy Communion and Related Rites. Renewing Worship, vol. 6 (2004).
> The primary pattern and rite for the weekly assembly around word and sacrament, together with supplemental materials and music for trial use.

Daily Prayer. Renewing Worship, vol. 7 (2004).
> Services of daily prayer for morning, evening, and the close of day, together with selected psalms and canticles and music for trial use.

The Church's Year: Propers and Seasonal Rites. Renewing Worship, vol. 8 (2004).
> Lectionary, calendar, seasonal texts for the Sunday assembly, and selected seasonal and holy day rites.

Ministry and the Church's Life. Renewing Worship, vol. 9 (2005).
> Occasional services related to ministry, the congregation, and other expressions of the church.

Evaluation

An essential goal of Renewing Worship is the use of provisional resources in worship and the evaluation of these resources by congregations and their leaders. Some congregations may use only a few of the rites in this volume, while others may use most or all of them. Included here as well as at www.renewingworship.org is a reproducible evaluation tool that can be used to evaluate any or all of the rites contained in *Life Passages: Marriage, Healing, Funeral.*

Evaluations for different rites may be submitted together or individually, at one time or over the course of several years, but please fill out a separate form for each rite. Be sure to include the completed last page of the evaluation with each submission.

Please place a check mark next to the rite you are evaluating (choose one rite only for each form):

Marriage
_____ Marriage

Healing
_____ Liturgy of Healing
_____ Commendation of the Dying
_____ Prayer When Life-sustaining Care Ends
_____ Confession and Forgiveness: Individual Order

Funeral
_____ Comforting the Bereaved
_____ Funeral Liturgy
_____ Committal

Please indicate your agreement with the statements that follow by circling the appropriate number. If desired, add comments to support your response.

1. The rite is faithful to scripture and the church's tradition.

    Agree   Disagree

    1   2   3   4   5

Comments:

2. The style and language of the rite is accessible to our worshiping assembly.

    Agree   Disagree

    1   2   3   4   5

Comments:

3. The rite is easy to follow and to adapt for our worshiping assembly.

    Agree   Disagree

    1   2   3   4   5

Comments:

4. The rite is useful in the life of our congregation.

    Agree   Disagree

    1   2   3   4   5

Comments:

5. Who was involved in the planning related to use of this rite?

____ Pastor(s)
____ Pastor(s) and other staff
____ Group of lay members with pastoral and other staff
____ Other (describe): _____

6. In what context was the rite used?

____ Within a regularly scheduled service of Holy Communion
____ Within another type of regularly scheduled service
____ Outside of a regularly scheduled service
____ As an occasional service in a particular pastoral circumstance
____ Studied but not used in worship
____ Other (describe): _____

7. How many times did you use the rite prior to this evaluation?_____

8. One of the goals of Renewing Worship is to provide options that can be used in flexible ways. Which statement best describes the options provided in this rite?

____ A sufficient number of options are provided with the rite.
____ Too many options are provided with the rite.
____ Too few options are provided with the rite.

9. Are there additional rites related to the rites in *Life Passsages: Marriage, Healing, Funeral* that should be included in final resources? Please describe.

10. Please note any additional comments and suggestions for improvement.

INFORMATION ABOUT THIS EVALUATION

Please provide the requested information and include it with each separately submitted evaluation, whether filled in on this form (or a photocopy of it) or in a letter.

ELCA Congregation ID # _____

If this response is not from an ELCA congregation or you do not know your congregation ID number, please note:

    Congregation: _____
    Location: _____
    Denomination: _____

Who prepared this evaluation?

Name: _____

I am: _____ Female _____ Male

I am: _____ Lay _____ Lay-rostered _____ Congregational pastor
    _____ Pastor in specialized ministry/retired

I am: _____ Paid staff _____ Volunteer staff _____ Not staff

I am: _____ American Indian or Alaska Native
    _____ Black or African American
    _____ Hispanic or Latino/a
    _____ Native Hawaiian or other Pacific Islander
    _____ White
    _____ Other: _____

I am: _____ Under 25 _____ 25–50 _____ 50–65 _____ over 65

Is this _____ a personal evaluation of the rites _____ a response to which a group has agreed?

Have you been part of a group that studied or discussed these rites? _____ Yes _____ No

What is the nature of this group?
_____ Congregation council or other congregational leadership
_____ Congregational study group made up primarily of lay people
_____ Group of congregational pastors and/or other rostered leaders
_____ Other (describe): _____

Please return the completed evaluation to Renewing Worship Evaluation, Division for Congregational Ministries, Evangelical Lutheran Church in America, 8765 West Higgins Road, Chicago, IL 60631.

ISBN 0806670045

9 780806 670041

90000